"As a biblical counsel(ge forty-two, I've seen ma :es regarding dating and marriage they later came to regret. It's my hope that the heartache experienced by many single women will be averted because of the wisdom Deepak offers in this book. Whether you're a single woman or not, you'll find this book is for you—because it's all about being grounded in Christ."

Amy Baker, Ministry Resource Director, Faith Church; Counselor at Faith Biblical Counseling Ministries; author of *Picture Perfect* and *Getting to the Heart of Friendships*

"Deepak has written a much-needed word to single women which is full of biblical truth and wisdom. His wealth of experience has given him the ability to write with understanding and conviction as he encourages young women to pursue Christ, patiently trust God's plan, and depend on his grace while they wait on him. I highly recommend this book full of prudent warnings, poignant examples and godly counsel to single women."

David and Sally Michael, Cofounder of Children Desiring God

"Dr. Reju has turned the topic of dating on its head with this insightful and thoughtful look at who not to marry. As a seasoned counselor and brother in Christ, he walks single Christian women through a methodical process of considering the dangers of settling. Using compelling case studies, Deepak carefully leads them to consider many biblical factors that are sometimes swept away as insignificant while encouraging smart women to be patient in waiting for God's best."

Mary K. Mohler, President's Wife, The Southern Baptist Theological Seminary; Director of Seminary Wives Institute

"With the wisdom that comes from hours and hours of counseling brokenhearted women, the biblical insight that springs from years in the Scriptures, and the compassion that flows out of the heart of a follower of Jesus, Deepak has written a sensitive and important book for women who want to be married and might be tempted to settle for someone . . . anyone . . . who will take away the loneliness. Sisters, if you're considering who you should date (and ultimately marry), let me encourage you to read this book first and to take Deepak's counsel to heart. He loves the Lord and his words are true."

Elyse Fitzpatrick, Author of *Counsel from the Cross: Connecting Broken People to the Love of Jesus*

"As I read *She's Got the Wrong Guy*, I kept thinking, 'This book is like a modern-day book of Proverbs written by a father to his young adult daughter.' Pastor Deepak Reju writes with compassionate gospel-centered, proverbial wisdom relevantly applying God's truth to the vital topic of singleness, dating, and marriage. This is the book that I'll be recommending to single women."

Bob Kellemen, Founder and CEO of RPM Ministries; author of *Gospel-Centered Counseling: How to Care Like Christ*

"*She's Got the Wrong Guy* is a wonderful book. I thoroughly enjoyed reading it. It is very God-honoring, practical, engaging, and convicting. I already know several women who could benefit from this book including my five granddaughters. As a biblical counselor to women, this book is an exceptional resource. I highly recommend it."

Martha Peace, Author of *The Excellent Wife* and *Biblical Counselor*

"Deepak Reju's *She's Got the Wrong Guy* peeks into many kinds of marriage misery. He describes how and why many Christian women choose poorly. Wise single women will read and be grateful for his astute observations and ability to pinpoint why these wrong guys might seem right—and why smart Christian women should avoid them."

Susan Olasky, Senior Writer, *World Magazine*

"Page by page of *She's Got the Wrong Guy* is full of convincing and convicting truth. Shared through stories, women will find the content exceptionally relatable. The book precisely conveys what a mature view of relationship should look like and why it desperately matters. It is a book for singles and a book for those in relationship who want solid biblical guidance."

Eliza Huie, Biblical Counselor at Life Counseling Center, Marriottsville, Maryland; author of *Raising Teens in a Hyper-Sexualized World*

"Deepak Reju has given us single women an engaging book full of relatable dating dilemmas and biblical wisdom for help. He identifies common warning signs that are not typically discussed in a Christian book on dating. Whether you're having doubts about a relationship or need encouragement to prioritize God's standards, read this book and share it with others."

Lilly Park, Counselor and Adjunct Professor

"This is a book that should have been written years ago. Gratefully, it's here in time for our four daughters, and you can be sure we will be reading this biblically wise and practical treatment with all of them. Single men, too, might read it to discover the kind of man parents like us pray for daily."

Jonathan and Shannon Leeman, Editorial director for 9Marks

"Tired of waiting for the right man to come along? Weary of delaying 'wedded bliss?' Are you tempted to redefine love so you can accommodate a lesser man in an okay marriage? Don't you dare. The cosmic stakes are too high and your life is too precious to settle for a second-best marriage. If you're looking for the emotional strength to wait well on God's man, my friend Deepak Reju has written the perfect guide in this remarkable book you hold in your hands. I give it a big double-thumbs up!"

Joni Eareckson Tada, Joni and Friends International Disability Center

"This book is important for women who are dating, but it also for their good friends who want to help, for men who don't want to be the wrong guy, and for anyone who loves someone who will be dating. Your pastor will be Deepak. He will speak to you like a father as you carefully consider one of life's most consequential decisions."

Ed and Sheri Welch, Counselor & Faculty Member CCEF; author

"There are very few books out there that deserve the 'must-read' status, and this is one of them. I want all of the single ladies in our church and our daughters to read this book. Deepak's wise counsel is both urgent and timely. Applying the principles in this book will certainly spare a whole lot of people unnecessary pain and lead readers to a greater understanding of what it means to make Jesus the center of everything."

Gloria Furman, Author of *Missional Motherhood* and *Alive in Him*

"This now, is the book I'll be recommending for single women who long for marriage. With tough but loving truth, Deepak disciples single women with pastoral care and brotherly protection in one of the best books I've read regarding dating and singleness. Every single man who desires to marry should read it too, as it's a roadmap for transformation into being a godly boyfriend and a Christ-like husband, or not."

Ellen Mary Dykas, Women's Ministry Director, Harvest USA; author/editor of *Sexual Sanity for Women* and *Sex and the Single Girl*

SHE'S GOT THE WRONG GUY

Why Smart Women Settle

Deepak Reju

New
Growth
Press

WWW.NEWGROWTHPRESS.COM

New Growth Press, Greensboro, NC 27404
Copyright © 2017 by Deepak Reju

Cover Design: Faceout Books, faceoutstudio.com
Typesetting: Lisa Parnell, lparnell.com

ISBN 978-1-945270-09-3 (Print)
ISBN 978-1-945270-10-9 (eBook)

Library of Congress Cataloging-in-Publication Data on file

Printed in the United States of America

24 23 22 21 20 19 18 17   1 2 3 4 5

Contents

PART 1:

From Problems to Faith

When it comes to dating and marriage, what problems do you face as a single woman? As you deal with these difficulties, can you learn to put your faith in Christ? We start with a simple thesis: in the midst of the contemporary challenges to dating and marriage, the greatest need for a single woman is to ground her life in Christ.

1
Same People, New Problems

Jacqueline sat on my couch, tears streaming down her face. Her latest relationship had just fallen apart. It's happened to her way too often. As a little girl, she watched Prince Charming waltz into the end of every Disney story, mesmerizing the beautiful princess, and dreamed, "One day that will be me." She was sure that one day she would be a wife and a mother. But here she was, crying over another severed relationship, and the pain was unbearable and raw.

Her dating relationships didn't last long enough to see her dreams fulfilled. The string of broken relationships hurt. She couldn't help but think,

What's wrong with me? Why wouldn't a guy pick me?
Does God care? Doesn't he know what I want?
Why does it have to hurt this much?
Am I going to be alone forever?
Am I never going to have children?

To be a single woman in the twenty-first century is challenging. Old mores about marriage and dating have fallen away. And it's all too easy to lose sight of the gospel in today's complex and confusing dating world. The pressures and pitfalls are real. Where is Jesus in the middle of this mess? Does he care? Will he remember me in my hardest, saddest, most scary moments?

Your challenges are not the same ones your parents faced. Online dating, confusion over gender and marriage, open acceptance of premarital sex and pornography—your momma and papa never encountered these problems, nor did they know how to prepare you.

Shifts in the Cultural Landscape of Dating

Consider some of the current challenges for any single, twenty-first-century woman who desires to be married:

Sex Is Everywhere

Look around you, and you'll find sex. Television and movies for sure, but it's really everywhere in our culture. Walk in any major populated area in the hot summer, and notice how people are dressed. Body parts are revealed to show almost everything. Get on your smart phone or tablet, or flip through a magazine; look at the billboards on the highway, or movie previews, and you'll find sleek women, attractively dressed, always happy, who send the not-so-subtle message, "Life is not good . . . unless you look like me."

The unspoken (and spoken) message from our culture is that to be in a dating relationship, and to make it last, a woman must have sex. "*Real* Christian men wouldn't do that to a woman," some might argue. Not true. I've counseled dozens of couples and heard an endless stream of confessions. Sexual promiscuity is everywhere, even among born-again, church-going, Jesus-loving, Bible-believing Christians.

To be sexy, to be attractive, to be alluring is the way to get a man's attention. Debbie complained to me, "When I was an overweight woman who loved the Lord, no one asked me out. When I got thin, guys started to pay attention." A woman who loves God and others just doesn't seem good enough for guys in our image-obsessed culture.[1]

The availability of pornography only adds to the problems. Porn addiction is a plague, affecting men and women alike. It's not just still-life images. Chat rooms, videos, and now, even virtual porn (viewing another person on a camera in real time) are readily available. This generation has grown up with the internet, and along the way they've been dragged through the mud, fighting against the plights and pitfalls of pornography consumption. Through pornography, men's and women's hearts are shaped to satisfy their ever-present sexual impulses, and to give in to their sexual urges. What does that do to relationships? It makes men and women think about relationships primarily in terms of self-fulfillment. It promotes unrealistic expectations. It erodes servant-hearted, self-sacrificial relationships. It makes relationships much less than what God intends for them to be.

It's Hard to Find Good Men

If we look at most churches on Sunday mornings, we will find many more women than men. A surplus of strong, godly women compared to the number of godly men means fewer choices for women and more choices for men. Men are pickier ("I want a *hot* wife"), and women often settle for less.

Where are the genuine, faithful, committed, hard-working, Christ-centered, self-sacrificing Christian men? A woman looks around her church and thinks, *All the good ones are already taken.*

Expectations for what a godly man looks like can change depending on the context. A scarcity of men can produce perilously low expectations—he listens to Christian radio, he regularly bathes, and is willing to go to church. That's good enough, right? In other situations, there are insurmountably high expectations—a humble man (who takes responsibility for his spiritual growth and serves in the church) is looked down upon because he doesn't have the *right* theology, or doesn't pray the *right* way, or doesn't know the *right* churchy language.

The Good and the Bad of Online Dating

Long gone are the days when a woman is restricted to her local church. Technology lets her have a relationship with anyone anywhere in the world. There are more options. More people. Better odds. So why not?

Worship the god of options, and you'll be overtaken by a consumer mentality. If a woman gets fifty choices of cereal, twenty types of ice cream, ten flavors of fruity drinks, and everything available in gluten-free or regular, why can't she get more than one choice in a man? As one young woman prayed in my office, "Give me what I want, or else, I'll hate you, God."

I've met many happily married couples who met online. Like everything else in life, if you are wise and thoughtful about how you approach it, online dating can be a great thing. But be careful of the dangers that lurk in the online world. An online persona is a very thin slice of a person's real life. Remove the context. Get a one-sided view of the person. Happy pictures. Good résumé. Witty banter. A woman gets quickly sucked in. Hope rises. Maybe he is the one?

A lack of community engagement removes the observations a woman can make when she sees a man in his church context. Is he a flirt or servant-hearted? Does he love the Word or is he all about himself? Is he ambitious for worldly things, or for Christ and his kingdom? It's hard to truly know a guy because the woman only sees him in a one-on-one context, where he can put his best foot forward, and hide all the rest.

Technology Changes the Way We Do Relationships

Nowadays, guys pay attention to women (and vice versa) on Facebook, Instagram, Twitter, Snapchat, and a whole host of social media platforms. A man and woman don't actually have to talk face-to-face to have a quasi-emotional relationship. They can talk via social media or communication apps, and not spend any tangible time in person.

There are new rules and new ways to play in the jungle. Texting is the new norm. Karen wrote me:

> "A guy can text a girl coy texts like, 'Wanna get coffee?' and the girl is left reeling with the question, 'Wait, did he ask me on a date, or is this just super impersonal and casual?' It raises questions like: 'He just liked my photo on Facebook and he doesn't like other photos from other girls—does that mean he's giving me attention and is interested?' or 'This guy keeps retweeting my tweets and liking my photos on Instagram—is he interested?'"

It's just too easy to hide behind a screen when having a "conversation." A guy gets a woman to be vulnerable with long texts with deeply personal questions, and the woman is left to either take the risk or lose the guy's interest. It's a lazy man's dream—no intentionality, no commitment, and no risk. He can text, tweet, or like her pictures all he wants and never face any accountability for his actions. Nobody is overseeing a guy's online behavior, so he can drift off into cyberspace whenever he loses interest, and the girl is left reeling. She asks, "What did I do wrong?" And he doesn't even have to answer!

More Educated, Accomplished, Confident Women

The reality is that today there are more educated, accomplished, and talented women in the workforce. Women finish college and pour themselves into a career in much higher numbers than previous generations. A man meets a successful woman, and it can be intimidating for him to ask her out. Women can sense this.

This leads to difficult questions as a woman sorts through her education and career choices: How do I pay my bills, pay for my life, and do my job with excellence without hurting my chances at getting married? Will a certain career path limit my chances of dating? Are there certain jobs that are less threatening to men? Do I have to be an elementary education teacher to attract a Christian man? Are men scared of my intelligence, career, or salary level?

The secular world often does a better job of valuing and positively reinforcing women for their intelligence, capability, and potential. Christian women are rewarded and affirmed at their jobs, but feel like second-class citizens in the church.

Dating is *not easy*. Dating as a conservative Christian woman is *hard*. Dating as an intelligent, gifted, and self-confident Christian woman *feels impossible*.

Single Longer and Married Later

In our day, there is a growing skepticism that marriages can really last. More people are gun-shy about marriage. Statistics bear this out—the CDC reports that the US marriage rate is falling and at an all-time low.[2] Fewer Americans are choosing to marry at all.

For those who do marry, the trend is to get married later in life, prioritizing independence, graduate education, and careers over marriage. The average age of marriage is at an historic high—twenty-seven for women and twenty-nine for men, jumping from a 1990 average of twenty-three for women and twenty-six for men.[3]

The message of Western culture to singles is to wait, to enjoy your freedom, and to try living together to see if things work out. Take this skepticism about marriage, add to it that those who are marrying do it later, and you're left with more Christians who stay single much longer than their parents did.

We're swimming in uncharted seas. Single Christians wrestle with questions of faithfulness as older believers living on their own. They fight for purity much longer, not just a few years after college, but for many, a decade or two. What it means to live faithfully in singleness for a longer period of time is a question that more people are facing than ever before.

You Are Not Alone

There are even more contemporary issues in dating, many of which I don't have space to write about—confusion over sexuality, gender, and marriage, and a rising number of divorced singles and single parents. Each of these is worthy of a book on its own. The challenges that Christian women face are not trivial; they're substantial, fraught with difficulty, and sometimes even tragedy.

If you currently feel overwhelmed by the confusing, complex, and often convoluted world of dating, please don't stop reading. You are not alone in this battle.

I've written this book because I want to help you wade knee-deep through the murky waters of the swamp and get out on the other side. The end result may not be what you had planned. One woman commented to me, "As Christian women, we teach the gospel, pray the gospel, sing the gospel—and we secretly hope for marriage."

Is marriage your paradise, your mecca, your ultimate dream?

Take a moment to examine your own heart. From the outset, it helps to be honest—as a woman, is your deepest desire for a husband, or for Christ? In a confusing world of dating, amongst the many challenges to women in the twenty-first century, *your starting point needs to be a clear dependence on Christ.* Jesus knows your challenges and your desire for a life partner, and he's not going to let you go it alone. Start with an honest heart that tells Jesus all about your struggles. Look to him for help. Jesus will help—it's a promise that's guaranteed (John 14:18).

2

Smart Women Settle

Rachel and Andrew

Rachel met Andrew at work. He was an engineer and she was an administrative assistant for one of the VPs of the company. They worked down the hallway from each other and talked often. Conversations drifted into lunches. Lunches turned into phone calls, texts, and eventually, hanging out on the weekends.

Everyone liked Andrew. He worked hard. He earned the respect of his colleagues. Rachel noticed. She was immediately attracted to him—tall, clean-cut, muscular build, clear blue eyes. He enjoyed hiking on the weekends when weather permitted. She cherished time with him, whether indoors or outdoors. He made her smile. She laughed with him. And they both craved a hefty jolt of caffeine in the morning.

Rachel grew up in a Christian home. She went to church and at an early age read the Bible on her own. In seventh grade, in a youth meeting, she felt convicted of her pride and selfishness, repented of her sins, and trusted in Christ. Though she had good days and bad days, on the whole, she persevered through the tumultuous teen years and emerged with a solid faith in Christ.

Andrew never went to church. He grew up in a nominal Christian home. He wasn't interested in God, and felt like if he worked hard in life, he'd do just fine. He studied, went to a decent college, and got a respectable job after graduation. He was drawn to Rachel as soon as he met her. She was outgoing and quick-witted. She was attractive, but even more so, she was a beautiful person, full of life and personality. Their relationship blossomed quickly.

Rachel's parents met Andrew. They liked him. It seemed to them like he was a considerate young man, but he had no interest in God. He never came to church. If he was present for family devotions, he didn't say a word. He respectfully listened to their conversations about Jesus, but he didn't seem interested.

Rachel's parents and her close Christian friends spoke to her about Andrew. They challenged her to find someone else, because it was clear that Andrew was not a believer. They showed her Bible texts and tried to convince her that the Bible directed her to marry a Christian man. Rachel knew this. Andrew was honest about his lack of faith, but she didn't want to give him up.

For as long as she could remember, she had always wanted to get married and be a mother. She had dated in high school, but the guys were immature and worldly. Andrew was caring, thoughtful, and hard working. Most of all, he loved her and from the very first day they hung out, he was nothing but supportive of her. Why would she give him up? Didn't they understand how good he was to her? She knew the Bible verses about dating an unbeliever—"do not be unequally yoked" (2 Corinthians 6:14) and you must marry "only in the Lord" (1 Corinthians 7:39). But it felt unreasonable, even unfair, that God (let alone her parents and friends) would want her to break up with Andrew. Her closest friends had husbands and children of their own. How could they deny her the same privilege?

Carol and Frank

Carol met Frank for the first time on a blind date. They had mutual friends who thought they would be good for each other. Frank thought it was worth a shot. Carol hadn't dated in two years, so she was eager to give it a try.

Initially, things were slow. On the first date, conversation was pleasant, but not very exciting. On the second date, Frank was more relaxed, and not so uptight. They laughed a good bit more. On the third date, he kissed her, and she *loved* it. No one had shown her physical affection in years, and she craved it like a little kid who longs for three scoops of Rocky Road ice cream on a scalding hot summer day.

Several months later, they got engaged, planned a wedding, and entered into marital bliss exactly a year after they met.

Carol became a Christian in college. Her parents were self-professed atheists, and didn't teach her any form of religion. Her freshman year, she had laughed at a girl who invited her to a Bible study, but she eventually went, and was surprised at God's grace. The thought that God would take all of her wrong away and give her freedom instead was inconceivable. Surely there was something she had to do to earn this? There had to be some catch? Some gimmick to get her to give money? Her Bible study leader kept on insisting, "Carol, grace is free. There is nothing you can do to earn it." As she read over the book of Ephesians one night in her dorm room, God's mercy for a sinner like herself overwhelmed her, and the next morning, she woke up confident of God's love for her.

Frank was a different story. He grew up in a very religious home, but the hypocrisy of his parents made him detest religion. His father and mother often put on a show at church, donning their best attire, and greeting others warmly. But his home life was like a medieval dungeon—his parents screamed and hit him, making him feel as if he was the reason why their life was miserable. "Stupid kid!" "What's wrong with you?" "How can you be such a loser?" If God existed, he'd given him the worst parents in the universe, just to show him that he didn't love him. Frank wanted nothing to do with a god like that. For years, Frank turned his back on God.

But to his surprise, one year after college, Frank's best friend became a Christian and started attending a Bible-believing church. He dragged Frank to church because he didn't want to go alone. Several weeks of biblically-rich sermons washed over him like a fresh mountain spring. God forgives. He loves. He hates evil. He brings justice against wrong. He even sent his Son to die for atheists like Frank. Ten weeks after starting to go to church, he gave his life to Christ, and it was one month later that his best friend set him up with Carol for a blind date.

Their marriage was hard. They fought often. Some fights lasted all afternoon. Frank would get very emotional, screaming at her, "I hate you!" "You are incompetent!" "Why don't you help me?" His anger erupted, like a volcano explosion, with lava destroying everything in its path. Carol either fought back, disengaged, or even walked out on him. "Don't you dare leave me again!" he'd bellow at her as she left. Carol didn't want to leave, but she didn't know how to cope with his rage.

He was an immature believer when they got married. His grip on Christ was not firm, and the mayhem in marriage made it hard to grow. She spent so much energy trying to survive the tumult, she had nothing left for Christ. How was she to know? Frank didn't even know himself why he was so angry. No one ever warned her about the dangers of marrying a brand-new convert.

Mary and Colby

Mary struggled with trusting God. Life was hard right now. It was exhausting to work full-time and be a single mom. Her life was not what she had ever expected.

Colby and Mary met on a blind date, and hit it off immediately. Most of their friends thought they were a wonderful match, so it didn't surprise anyone that they married quickly. In the midst of the romance and the quick engagement, she ignored warning signs. He was often a flirt with other women, but he just passed it off as harmless. They fell several times into premarital sex, and despite her pleas to stop transgressing the forbidden lines, it didn't stop. But she pressed on because she loved Colby and she desperately wanted to get married.

So Mary was devastated when Colby broke the news. After ten years of marriage, Colby confessed to a two-year affair with a woman at work. They went to their pastor for counseling. Weeks of crying, hard conversations, and accountability followed. She did what a Christian does in turmoil—she prayed, read her Bible, and leaned on close friends. In the end, Colby said he didn't love her anymore, and wanted out. He packed a bag and left her. A week later, he moved in with his lover. Six months later, they were divorced.

Her pastor, his wife, and several Christian friends walked through the darkest moments with Mary. They did what they could to answer her hard questions—"God, where are you?" "How could you do this to me?" "Don't you love me?" "Don't you love my son, Tyler? Shouldn't he have a stable family?" "What did I do wrong?" "What's wrong with me that Colby would leave me?"

Shattered dreams. Broken hopes. Lonely nights. Too many fears.

Mary continued to go to church, but it was hard to trust the Lord. Some days it felt like God had betrayed her even more than Colby had. Her friends and pastor walked with her as she fought for faith through the difficulties.

After the divorce, she returned to the workforce and put Tyler in school. Most days she came home exhausted and used what energy was left to get him to bed as soon as possible. After that, she did what she had to (dishes, laundry, bills), went to sleep, and started all over again the next day.

She hated the thought of starting to date again. Single women at church did nothing but complain about the available men. She knew how hard dating could be. It was fraught with emotional pitfalls, and she just didn't have much to give. Who would want a divorced, single mom anyway? Probably no one.

A Christian Woman's Dilemma

Rachel, Carol, and Mary are not alone. Their dilemma is fairly common. A single woman gives her life to Christ. She pursues the life of a Christian—reading her Bible, going to church, listening to sermons, and cultivating Christian friendships. Along the way, she holds onto her dreams of becoming a wife and a mother one day. The Bible tells her that both are good desires to have (Proverbs 31:28). She doesn't know how or when they might come to fruition.

Enter, stage left: The man.

There are some significant things about him she'd rather change, but overall, she likes him. She decides to put up with his flaws in order to hold onto him. She *settles*, and joins a host of other women like her—smart women—who have dated and married these men in their quest for marriage and motherhood.

Rachel wanted to marry a Christian man, but none came along. And there was so much to like about Andrew, she wasn't willing to give him up.

Carol married an immature Christian man. At least he professed Christ and went to church. He held a decent job and showed her kindness, so she couldn't ask for much more.

Mary married a Christian man from church who turned out to be an adulterer. She lamented that she had ignored all of the warning signs— he often flirted with other women and demanded sex before they were married.

It's easy to point a finger at these women and say, "Bad choice. You should have known better." You might even think, *When it's my turn, I won't make the same mistakes.* Really? Talk to a few wives in your church and you'll find out how many struggle in marriage. Even better, call the pastor and ask him how many marriages he is concerned about in the church.

Rachel, Carol, and Mary all settled, and ended up in marriages they never expected. Now they are living with the consequences of their choices, and battle daily to live by faith. Christ will meet them in their struggle, and walk the hard, confusing road with them. He will never abandon them, but will continue to write the stories of their lives. The storyline may not be what they expected, but they take comfort that Jesus is the author.

What about you? If you are still single, your choice has not yet been finalized. What would lead you to settle? In this complex and difficult world of dating, the fact is that many Christian women do settle. But *why?* Why do smart, faithful, godly Christian women settle and end up in these difficult situations? That's the subject of our next chapter.

3
Why Do Smart Women Settle?

I was sitting in my office, talking with a woman whose marriage was a wreck. Her husband was lying. Their daily conversations often spiraled into nuclear war. Her resentment was growing. There was no peace, and she was holding off the possibility of divorce, but you could sense it hovering like a dark cloud.

At one point she said to me, "When we were dating, he never initiated spiritual conversations and we never talked about the Bible. I just figured that things would change *after* we got married." I just about fell out of my chair, carefully lifting my jaw off the floor. You thought he would become more spiritual after you got married?

I wasn't angry or judgmental when she shared that. I was simply sad. In my experience as a pastor, I've seen single women make many similar mistakes. I feel for them as they sit in my office and ask themselves (and me) an important question: Why was I willing to settle? Why did I push down my doubts and pick the "wrong" guy?

Why Women Choose the Wrong Guy

There are reasons why single women settle. Consider a few that I have witnessed firsthand in my counseling office.

Putting Marriage First

My girls are just entering elementary school, but you can already see the initial stages of them thinking that getting married is the most important thing in life. Every episode of Ken and Barbie ends in a happy marriage. Playtime often includes a wedding ceremony (where their brother is forced to be the pastor or the groom). Disney movies end with the prince giving the princess a long kiss. It only continues as they grow up: a teenage interest in boys springs up, Hollywood rom-coms fuel dreams of romance, and even Christian fiction is packed with love stories. Add to this how churches (rightfully) teach a high view of marriage, and how within a few years of college graduation most of their closest friends will pair off with boyfriends and get married.

Is it any surprise that Christian women grow up idealizing marriage? And that sometimes they allow that good desire to become the most important thing in their life? The Bible uses an old-fashioned word to describe a desire that has taken center stage in our lives—idolatry. It might be hard to understand how that applies to the desire to be married, but stay with me. This is important.

Idolatry happens anytime we make something God created more important than God himself. The apostle Paul explains this in Romans 1:25: "They exchanged the truth about God for a lie and worshiped and served the creature rather than the Creator." Everyone does this by nature. We know the truth of God but we choose to replace it with a lie. We serve what God made rather than worship him who made all things.

At its core, idolatry is worshipping something created rather than the Creator. It is elevating it (whatever "it" is) to a status it never deserved. When it comes to marriage, idolatry looks like building your hopes, dreams, and goals around getting married and of course, living happily ever after.

The institution of marriage was never meant to carry this kind of importance. In and of itself, marriage is a temporary good. In heaven, there will be no marriage (Matthew 22:29–33); and our focus will be on God, the one who made all things (Genesis 1; Isaiah 44:24; 66:2), including marriage. And yet from an early age, many girls develop an idolatry of marriage that gives birth to full-blown lies: "Happiness is found in marriage," "I won't be satisfied until I find a good guy," or "If God loves me, he'll give me a husband."

The Bible commends the desire to be married and says that a godly spouse is a good gift from God (Proverbs 18:22; James 1:17). But for many women I've counseled, these good *desires* morph into *demands*. A woman may never use theological terms like "idolatry" or "worship," but her thoughts and emotions reveal what's going on in her heart (Luke 6:43–47). When her closest friends get married and her dating relationships are not going anywhere, her disappointment and fear take center stage. From there it's easy to question God and wonder: *Does God love me? Why doesn't anyone notice me? Does God want me to be alone forever?* Her doubts about God's goodness to her reveal that her hope is in marriage and not in God.

Personal Baggage

Women also settle because of their past experiences. Every woman has a past, and much like a well-prepared traveler, she carries plenty of personal baggage on her adventures. What does she carry into her dating relationships?

Maybe it is the you-complete-me syndrome, where there is no sense of personal identity apart from relationships with men. Perhaps her fear of rejection is so overwhelming that she doesn't feel worthy unless a man finds her worthy of his attention.

Some of her luggage might be crammed with poor role models. Her parents fought all of the time, and ended up divorced. Everyone she knows is divorced. She can't think of a single marriage that goes the distance.

Others internalize convoluted messages from family, friends, or the culture about what relationships are for, what she should look for in a man, and how to get into a relationship. Here are a few lies that might be impacting her:

- "You can't have a relationship with a guy without having sex. It's just not the way it works."
- "You'll never find a decent man if you don't look like a model."
- "It's better to hide what you really think and what you really want in a relationship with a guy."

Adding to these distorted messages is the reality that many women have been abused. It's difficult for them to form an honest, open relationship with a guy. Often they are simply afraid to believe that good men do exist.

Love Is Blind

Sometimes smart women settle because when it comes to relationships, they have blinders on. I don't usually like clichés, but "love is blind" often holds true. It might start out with something small. Janet told me how her then soon-to-be husband used to leave the orange juice out on the counter and forget to put it back in the fridge. She said, at the time, she thought it was "cute." After marriage, it grated on her. Her perspective changed. She was no longer blind to his little mistakes because she started to run into them more often. Of course, leaving the juice out is a small oversight and we all make mistakes. And love does overlook many faults. But what happens when you overlook a more serious issue? And you overlook it because you are afraid to lose your relationship? That's when "love is blind" becomes a serious problem.

If a woman lets herself get emotionally attached to the wrong kind of guy, principles that she thought she would never compromise on—like looking for a mature, godly man—no longer are her first priority. Because the relationship is fun, the guy is courteous and kind, and he pays attention like no one else will, a woman lets her priorities slide. It doesn't matter that he calls himself a "Christian," but doesn't go to church regularly. Or maybe he is an atheist or agnostic. Because she is growing more attached to this guy, she downplays or ignores that his lack of Christian values poses a barrier to the relationship. The woman's "blindness" is deliberate because she desperately desires to be married.

Lone-Ranger Dating

Because dating is difficult, it's easy for a single woman to think that she should simply take control. So she finds a man and makes things happen. God's not in the business of making matches; that's *her* job. She'll find the right guy. No one else will do that for her.

Her closest advisors are a few single friends. Their advice is no wiser than her own. She is open to talking with married folks, but they are busy and she's afraid of being a burden. Instead she defaults to dealing with dating issues by herself or by talking to a few single girlfriends.

Her overall approach to dating is no different than a lone-ranger cowboy wandering the Wild West—no map to guide her, nothing but her own wit and intellect to rely on, hoping upon hope that she won't run into trouble. She'll figure it out, right?

Fear

Some women live under the tyranny of their anxiety. Ann hates that fear rules her life. She's heard the Bible texts on worry: "Can any one of you by worrying add a single hour to your life?" (Matthew 6:27 NIV) and "Cast your anxiety on him because he cares for you" (1 Peter 5:7 NIV). None of these texts seem to make a difference. She wrestles with fears constantly.

- She's scared that she will be lonely for the rest of her life.
- She's afraid that she won't ever have children.
- She is fearful that no one will take care of her when she is old or feeble.

- She is nervous that once she turns thirty, or worse, forty, her chances at marriage will be nonexistent.
- She is worried that she won't be loved for who she is.
- She's concerned that others will look down on her for not having a relationship.
- She's fearful that others will see her as defective or not competent to make her own decisions.
- She's troubled that others will think she is too picky.
- She's scared that she will get her hopes up only to be hurt again.
- She's worried that not having a relationship means she's not worthy of one.
- She's very fearful that she will never have what she most wants.

Fear of man, fear of failure, fear of discomfort or suffering or difficulty, fear of not getting what she wants—it's all there. Because the fears own her heart, they also own her life.

Unhelpful, Ungodly Attitudes

A single woman's attitude toward dating and marriage can make all the difference in whom she picks, dates, and marries. Persistently wrong attitudes lead to poor choices.

Maybe a woman has a chameleon-like disposition. Her colors change with different men. She'll be whatever the man wants her to be, as long as he loves her.

Some women are fatalists. Their fathers were passive, or mean, or angry to their mother. Their boyfriends are not much different. So they assume that there is nothing better than this kind of man. They might say, "What's the point of trying to find a good relationship? It'll just end up the same way."

Others choose to blindly follow. Maybe they are naïve. Maybe they are desperate. What he wants, she'll do. This is what everyone says she should do, so that's what she'll do.

Some women are exceedingly hard on themselves. If we were to overhear their inner dialogue, we'd witness constant self-flagellation. She settles for a guy who is a jerk because she thinks that she doesn't deserve any better.

Quite a few women are determined to get what they want in life. They are confident, successful, and accomplished in their careers. If they are successful in the world's eyes, why can't they get what they want in dating and marriage? They apply the same attitude toward marriage, thinking, *I will get what I want no matter what.*

Looking for the Wrong Things

My wife handed me a notecard the other day. It was nestled between the pages of a used book that came in the mail.

The good physical traits of a potential husband

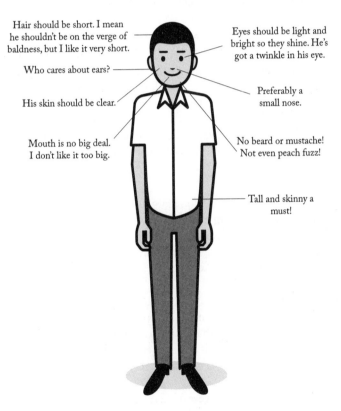

Hair should be short. I mean he shouldn't be on the verge of baldness, but I like it very short.

Who cares about ears?

His skin should be clear.

Mouth is no big deal. I don't like it too big.

Eyes should be light and bright so they shine. He's got a twinkle in his eye.

Preferably a small nose.

No beard or mustache! Not even peach fuzz!

Tall and skinny a must!

What does this notecard say about what this woman wants in a man? Everyone's got a list. The woman who drew this picture had one. You have one. On this woman's list were some very specific physical attributes. The guy had to have short hair, but he couldn't be balding. He needed to be well-built, etc., etc.

In church, everyone talks about godliness. But if we're honest, physical attraction really matters. A woman might not say it or admit it, but godly men who are balding, short, or have potbellies, don't get first consideration. They don't even make the list.

Add a few other important criteria for most women: He needs to be successful. He needs to be well-educated. He needs to be caring, sensitive, and thoughtful. He needs to make her feel special. He has to be romantic and well-built. He doesn't need to be perfect, but he needs to be a good catch, or else a woman's not going to waste her time.

What's Behind All of These Reasons for Settling?

If you pull back the curtain, you'll find that for many a Christian woman, when it comes to finding a relationship, God is no longer center stage in her life. Her fears and desires show what's most important to her. All too often when it comes to relationships, her small kingdom—the kingdom of "what I want out of life"—is really what matters most.

Surely there is a better way to find a spouse. A godless venture won't produce Christ-glorifying results. But what will?

Don't Forget Jesus

The answer is as simple as "don't forget Jesus." In your dreams, desires, hopes, and wishes, don't forget your first love—the one who is for you and promises to be with you through all the ups and downs of life. Don't let your desires or the values of this world take you away from your first love. The apostle Paul explains it like this:

> I am jealous for you with a godly jealousy. I promised you to one husband, to Christ, so that I might present you as a pure virgin to him. But I am afraid that just as Eve was deceived by the serpent's cunning, your minds may somehow be led astray from your sincere and pure devotion to Christ. (2 Corinthians 11:2–3 NIV)

Paul is describing the process of *betrothal*, which was a common practice in his day. Think of betrothal as equivalent to a modern-day engagement, but with legal boundaries. A woman was betrothed to a man a year before they said their marital vows and moved in with one another. After betrothal, a man and woman formally and legally belonged to one another, such that if either had an affair, it was a punishable offense. The father's responsibility was to watch over his daughter and preserve her purity in the year-long waiting period.

Paul makes an analogy with the Corinthian Christians—he (as their father figure) had betrothed them to Christ, and wanted to preserve them until the day when Christ returned to be with his bride. Just like the Corinthians, *a woman must always remember that her first love (whether she is single or married) must be Christ.* According to the apostle Paul, she is married to Christ!

Just as Eve was deceived by the serpent, so also Paul was fearful that the Corinthians would be led astray from their commitment to Christ. Paul's opponents were teaching them about a different Jesus, a different spirit, and a different gospel (v. 4). As a father figure to them, Paul was jealous for their spiritual well-being, just like a father would be for his own daughter.

What about you? What distracts you from Christ? What tempts you and leads you astray from a "sincere and pure devotion to Christ?" Has your desire to be married become a distraction from sincerely following Christ? Does your fear, unhelpful attitude, personal baggage, or emotional attachment to a guy keep you preoccupied with the wrong things? If this is true for you, then your goal needs to be to (first) renew your relationship with Christ and (second) find a better way to think about dating and marriage.

Ask yourself two crucial questions:

1. Do I desire Jesus more than anything else?
2. Would I settle for the wrong guy?

Ask the first question ("Do I desire Jesus more than anything else?") because if you are a Christian, *your relationship with Jesus should matter more than anything else in your life* (Philippians 3:8–11). Ask the second question ("Would I settle for the wrong guy?") so you can learn from the mistakes that others have made. As you work through the remaining chapters, test your own heart and be honest about where you see yourself in the pages of this book.

Everything we are going to talk about in one way or another will revolve around these two questions.

4

A New Direction—Living by Faith in Your Relationships

Janelle was single and lonely. The constant refrain in her heart was, "If only I had a man . . ."

If only I had a man, I'd be happy.

If only I had a man, I'd be able to have children.

If only I had a man, I'd have someone to be intimate with.

If only I had a man, I'd have a beautiful home, a white picket fence, and a dog.

If only I had a man, I'd have a future.

If only I had a man, I'd feel more secure in my life.

If only I had a man, I wouldn't have to make decisions on my own.

If only I had a man, I wouldn't have to go to weddings or do grocery shopping by myself.

If only I had a man, I'd have someone to rely on when I'm sick or old.

If only I had a man, I'd have someone to help me when I'm worried.

If only I had a man, I wouldn't be so lonely.

And the list goes on and on.

Does this same refrain ("If only I had a man . . .") reverberate in your life?

Spend a few minutes on any dating or wedding website, and you'd think that the mere presence of a man will make all your dreams come true. Picture this typical camera shot: A beautiful couple, staring longingly into each other's eyes, with perfectly combed hair, distinct facial features, sharp outfits, and panoramic scenery in the background. All of this is meant to create an illusion for you—get a man, and your life will be better, regardless of what it is like right now.

But it's worth taking a step back from that picture to consider if a man (any man) should be the focus of your life. Is a relationship with a man where true satisfaction lies? Our culture's message to single women is that their happiness matters more than anything else. Have you bought into this happiness mentality, by thinking, *If it makes me happy, it must be right* or *Surely God wouldn't want me to be miserable?*

As a Christian, your focus and call is to grow closer to Jesus—not to find a man.

The quest for *true* happiness starts by offering your heart and your life to Christ.

Real Treasures

Your ultimate solution to all those "if onlys" is not in finding a man. True satisfaction in this life doesn't come through earthly treasures, not even the gift of a godly husband. Jesus once said:

> "Do not lay up for yourselves treasures on earth, where moth and rust destroy and where thieves break in and steal, but lay up for yourselves treasures in heaven, where neither moth nor rust destroys and where thieves do not break in and steal. For where your treasure is, there your heart will be also." (Matthew 6:19–21)

A treasure is something that we cherish, long for and value. Jesus's warning is to not build your life around earthly treasures because they are temporary and perishable (v. 19). Instead, he says to focus your time, energy, and effort on heavenly treasures—things that will last; things that have no expiration date; things that can't be stolen by thieves or destroyed by moths or rust (v. 20).

In the Bible, the heart is the center of who you are. From it flow your thoughts, desires, emotions, and choices. Solomon considers your heart to be so vital that he warns, "Above all else, guard your heart for everything you do flows from it" (Proverbs 4:23 NIV). Jesus's concluding statement in verse 21 says that what matters to you most—what you cherish and value—will control your heart (and your life). If your greatest desire is for a husband, your heart will be bound up in pursuing that goal, while your pursuit of Christ will be secondary.

A husband, children, house, money in a retirement account, and other earthly goods are all wonderful to have, but they won't last. Devote yourself to these temporary treasures, and you devote yourself to time-limited and tentative things. Is that what you want? Why not pursue something that is eternal?

What you hope in matters. There are lots of wrong places to put your ultimate hopes (Lamentations 4:17–20; Psalm 20:7 NIV "Some trust in horses or chariots, but we trust in the name of the LORD our God"). A spouse is a good gift from God (James 1:17), but even those of us who are married know we can't put our ultimate hope in *who* we married.

Your hope cannot be in a husband, hypothetical or real. Your hope must be in the only person who will never fail you—Jesus Christ. Do you doubt whether God loves you, because he hasn't fulfilled your good desire for a husband and children? Remember the cross. God has already demonstrated his steadfast love for you by sending Christ. While you were still a sinner, an enemy of God, Christ died for you (Romans 5:8). A wedding ring does not prove God's love for you—the cross of Calvary does.

God *has not* promised you a husband or marriage in this life. He *has* promised that if you belong to him, you are part of his bride, the church (Revelation 19:7), and he is preparing a home for you that will last forever (John 14:2).

God *has not* promised that the man of your dreams will pursue you. He *has* promised that he will love you with a perfectly faithful, steadfast, and undying love (Exodus 34:6; 2 Thessalonians 3:4–5). God has already pursued you with perfect love by sending his Son to die in your place.

God *has not* promised that you will have children, but he *has* adopted you as his own beloved child (Romans 8:15). Jesus Christ himself is sharing his inheritance with you (Romans 8:17).

He *has not* promised you a man to grow old with, but he *has* promised you that he will never leave you or forsake you (John 14:18). He will never abandon you. He will be with you through every trial, every heartache, and every joy (Romans 8:38–39; John 16:33; Matthew 28:20). There is no burden that you will face that is too heavy for him to carry (Psalms 68:19; 94:18–19; 1 Peter 5:7). He made the universe, and he upholds it (Colossians 1:15–17). The same power that raised Jesus from the dead is at work in you (Ephesians 1:19–20). Will you trust Jesus with your uncertain future and believe that he is enough?

Treasure Christ. Hope in him. Don't build your heart around temporary treasures, like marriage to a godly husband, raising children, or the dream of a future together. Let your heart be captivated with Christ. Make Christ your greatest of all treasures.

Those Perilous Needs and Desires

What you think you need, and what you actually need, might be two different things. Your heart tells you that you need a husband and children to be happy. God tells you those are good gifts to *desire*, but what you really *need* is Christ. Take a moment and reflect on what rules your heart today.

Do you resent God for withholding marriage from you? Do you look at married couples with envy, and feel like God has forgotten you? Remember that in Christ you lack no good thing. You have everything you need for life and godliness, and you are secure with Christ forever. No threat of adultery, bank failure, disease, or even death can touch the good that God has secured for you in Christ. Jesus Christ has already died, and he will never die again. He always lives to intercede for you. You lack no good thing if you have Christ. Ask for the faith to believe that.

Instead of worrying about how to put yourself in the path of an eligible man, put yourself in the path of Jesus and listen to him. Many years ago, a Samaritan woman thought her day held just another ordinary trip out to draw water from the village well. Instead, she had a life-changing encounter with Jesus himself:

> So he came to a town of Samaria called Sychar, near the field that Jacob had given to his son Joseph. Jacob's well was there; so Jesus, wearied as he was from his journey, was sitting beside the well. It was about the sixth hour.
>
> A woman from Samaria came to draw water. Jesus said to her, "Give me a drink." (For his disciples had gone away into the city to buy food.)
>
> The Samaritan woman said to him, "How is it that you, a Jew, ask for a drink from me, a woman of Samaria?" (For Jews have no dealings with Samaritans.)
>
> Jesus answered her, "If you knew the gift of God, and who it is that is saying to you, 'Give me a drink,' you would have asked him, and he would have given you living water."
>
> The woman said to him, "Sir, you have nothing to draw water with, and the well is deep. Where do you get that living water? Are you greater than our father Jacob? He gave us the well and drank from it himself, as did his sons and his livestock."
>
> Jesus said to her, "Everyone who drinks of this water will be thirsty again, but whoever drinks of the water that I will give

him will never be thirsty again. The water that I will give him will become in him a spring of water welling up to eternal life."

The woman said to him, "Sir, give me this water, so that I will not be thirsty or have to come here to draw water." (John 4:5–15)

Jesus stopped at a town called Sychar, near the plot that Jacob had given his son (Genesis 48:22), and near a well which Jacob himself had dug. We see the human side of Jesus; he was tired from the journey and the midday heat and needed to sit down.

A Samaritan woman came to draw water, and Jesus showed no hesitation in speaking to her. This surprised the woman, who asked Jesus, "You are a Jew and I am a Samaritan woman. How can you ask me for a drink?" John's parenthetical comment ("For Jews do not associate with Samaritans") reflects the cultural and theological animosities that existed between Jews and Samaritans. Christ was not bound by worldly restrictions or prejudices, so he had no hesitation in engaging the Samaritan woman. He defied two Jewish restrictions—strict Jews would not have bought food from a Samaritan, for fear of defilement. Even worse, Samaritan women were considered to be perpetually in a state of ceremonial uncleanness, so it was doubly bad that Jesus not only spoke to a Samaritan, but also to a woman.[1]

Jesus asked her, "Will you give me a drink?" Because of the Jewish cultural and religious restrictions, she was understandably surprised. But we see that Jesus didn't care about the social and religious taboos of his day; he'd come to earth with a mission: to save sinners, no matter what the cost. She responded, "How can you (a Jew) ask me (a Samaritan woman) for a drink?" She was shocked. She couldn't fathom why a Jew would ask her for a drink.

Jesus answered by pointing to himself. "If you knew . . . *who it is* that asks you for a drink." If she knew who Jesus was, she would be asking him for living water (v. 10)—the eternal life that Christ provided through the Spirit.[2]

At this point, the woman did not understand what Jesus was saying. She didn't get the spiritual significance of the term "living water." She thought Jesus was talking about natural water. Not surprisingly, she asked how he could draw water from a hundred feet down when he had no bucket. Jacob dug the well and used materials to draw from the well. If Jesus could provide water without digging or using anything to draw water out, then surely he was greater than Jacob and Jacob's sons.

Jesus attempted to clear up her confusion. "Anyone who drinks natural water *from this well* will thirst again. But anyone who drinks from the water *I give* will never be thirsty again." He was contrasting physical thirst and spiritual thirst. Our physical thirst (v. 13) for water is never satisfied. No matter how much water the woman drew from the natural well, she would be thirsty again. Spiritual thirst (v. 14), on the other hand, is not a thirst for natural water, but a thirst for God. If the woman would only turn to Jesus and receive his free gift of eternal life, through his Spirit, she would be satisfied forever.

But she still didn't get it. She thought he was talking about physical water, as indicated by her desire to no longer have to "keep coming here to draw water." She was attracted to the idea of never being thirsty again, and so she asked for the water.

She thought she only needed physical water to satisfy her body's thirst. But what she really needed was Jesus. She needed to desire him first, because he alone could satisfy her forever. Natural water might seem to satisfy for a time, but she would only be thirsty again. Jesus pointed to what truly satisfies. Not physical water, but himself.

What is there for you in the Samaritan woman's encounter with Jesus? Start with your "thirsts." Think about all of your desires that you want to be satisfied—your thirst for a husband and children, for love and companionship, for future security and acceptance. Recognize that securing a husband might alleviate your thirst for a time, but you will be thirsty again. Nothing that this world has to offer, no matter how good the desire may seem, can satisfy your deepest need—your need for Christ. So don't set your heart on the water that won't satisfy. Turn your affections and desires to Christ, to make him first in your life.

Let your neediness be the platform for Christ to work in your life, revealing those desires that would tempt you to stray from him. Take your neediness and turn it into an exhibition of God's provision. Display to the world what a faithful, loving, tenderhearted provider you serve. Be satisfied in Christ. Build your life around Jesus, and root all of your needs in him.

Delight in Christ

Are you approaching this whole area of dating and marriage on your terms—"God give me what I want and I'll be happy"—or on God's terms? You can have an amazing ally in God if you are willing to come to him *on his terms*. What does God want for you? He wants you to delight in his Son.

Let's return to John's gospel and Jesus's encounter with the woman at the well.

> Jesus said to her, "Go, call your husband, and come here." The woman answered him, "I have no husband."
> Jesus said to her, "You are right in saying, 'I have no husband'; for you have had five husbands, and the one you now have is not your husband. What you have said is true."
> The woman said to him, "Sir, I perceive that you are a prophet. Our fathers worshiped on this mountain, but you say that in Jerusalem is the place where people ought to worship."
> Jesus said to her, "Woman, believe me, the hour is coming when neither on this mountain nor in Jerusalem will you worship the Father. You worship what you do not know; we worship what we know, for salvation is from the Jews. But the hour is coming, and is now here, when the true worshipers will worship the Father in spirit and truth, for the Father is seeking such people to worship him. God is spirit, and those who worship him must worship in spirit and truth."
> The woman said to him, "I know that Messiah is coming (he who is called Christ). When he comes, he will tell us all things."
> Jesus said to her, "I who speak to you am he." (John 4:16–26)

Jesus shifted the subject from living water to the woman's husband. He knew her sin and gently exposed it. He told her to go call her husband. She tried to fend off any further probing with the curt response, "I have no husband." Christ handled this sensitive subject graciously by commending her at first—"You are right when you say you have no husband." Technically, she didn't have a husband right then, because the former had either divorced her or died, and the current man in her life was someone she lived with, but was not married to. Jesus ended by confirming her statement: "What you have just said is true."

Why the abrupt change in subject? What did her husband have to do with the living water? Jesus knew her heart, and he could see that she did not yet understand who he was. She didn't see that her deepest and most significant needs were for Christ and eternal life. So Jesus made a second attempt to help her. He exposed her messed up life in order to help her grasp her deeper needs—not physical water, nor a husband, but a Savior who could take away her sins.

This woman built her life around being with men. She satisfied her longings with five men, and finally with one she didn't even marry. How many times do you think she said the words, "If only I had a man . . . "

Jesus displayed his omnipotence by telling the women about her life with five husbands without having to ask any questions. She was surprised, and she now saw she was not dealing with a mere man. She responded, "I see that you are a prophet." She recognized Jesus as someone with special insight into her life.

The Samaritan woman changed the subject in order to distract from the uncomfortable probing of her relationships (v. 18). She introduced a theological controversy about the proper place for worship. Should God's people worship in Jerusalem, as the Jews argued, or at Mount Gerazim, as the Samaritans held?

Jesus used her shift in subject to direct the conversation once more to the question of who he was, and what a person's response to him ought to be. Jesus argued that *where* one worships is a much less significant question than *who* is a true worshipper. With Jesus's death and resurrection looming ("the hour is coming"), arguments about Jerusalem and Mount Gerazim just wouldn't matter anymore (v. 21).

True worship of the Father is to occur "in spirit and truth" (v. 23). God's children worship God "in spirit" because he has put his Spirit in them. They worship God "in truth" because the Father has revealed himself through his Son. True worshippers are those who know the Son and are born of the Spirit.

The truth that "God is spirit" (v. 24) is significant because it helps us to see what God is like. He doesn't have a body, so he is not restricted to one location like human beings. Because he can't be confined to one place of worship, he can be worshipped anywhere.[3]

We can summarize Jesus's words: "At my death and resurrection, and even right now, because of my life and ministry, true worship of God, the Father, will occur because people have come to know me, the Son, and consequently, God has put his Spirit in them. God is spirit and he will not be restricted to specific location, but in fact, he will seek you out."

The woman seemed to understand enough of what Jesus was saying to see some of the messianic implications. She responded, "I know that Messiah" (called Christ) "is coming." These theological questions would be answered by the Messiah who would "explain everything" when he came. Little did she know that the Messiah was standing right in front of her.

If the woman had begun to suspect the truth, her comments about the Messiah (v. 25) may have been a confession of sorts in order to test what the Jewish stranger might say. Jesus needed no further invitation; he made it abundantly clear that he was the Messiah of whom she spoke (v. 26).

The men she had devoted her life to were nothing more than natural water that would never satisfy, but only leave her thirsty for more. Standing in front of her was God himself—the one who could change her life forever, the living water that would completely satisfy her. If she would put her trust in Jesus Christ, the Messiah, he would rescue her from her slavery to sin, and give her eternal life with him.

Is Jesus *your* Messiah? Has he rescued you from your selfish desires? Has he saved you not just from the world and the devil but from yourself (Ephesians 2:1–3)? The apostle Paul reminds us that Christ died so that "those who live might no longer live for themselves but for him who for their sake died and was raised" (2 Corinthians 5:15).

Your fundamental identity has nothing to do with your marital status. It has everything to do with this central question of whether or not you are trusting in Jesus as your Messiah, Savior, and Lord. The best way to find a husband is not to search for a man, but to fall in love with your Savior. Trust in Christ. Make him your priority. How do you do that? Start by turning away from any idols in your life, whether they are idols of security, happiness, comfort, marriage, sex, or companionship, and give your life fully over to Jesus.

If you are genuinely trusting in Christ and making him Lord over every aspect of your life, it will be shown in what you worship and treasure in this life. Does your life show, with every fiber of your being, that you really trust in him? Does your life demonstrate an increasing desire to grow in the Christian life? Are you studying the Bible, finding a godly person to disciple you, joining a gospel-preaching church, and committing to build your life around Jesus?

The most important ingredient of a happy life is not finding a husband, but in giving your life to Christ. Make Jesus your greatest treasure. Let your beauty not just be outward; let it be an inner beauty of a loving heart that doesn't fade (1 Peter 3:3–4). Pour yourself into loving Christ and let your love for him overflow in loving and serving the people around you. The best way to prepare for your future is to focus on becoming a woman whose greatest desire is Christ.

A Woman's Life Transformed

The woman at the well encountered Christ, and she was never the same again:

> So the woman left her water jar and went away into town and said to the people, "Come, see a man who told me all that I ever did. Can this be the Christ?" They went out of the town and were coming to him. (John 4:28–30)

In her excitement, the woman ironically left the water jar behind, and rushed to bear witness to the townspeople whom her shameful life gave her every reason to avoid.[4] She pled with them to come meet Jesus. Her statement—"a man who told me all that I ever did"—is probably one of hyperbole, but conveys how much she was affected by her brief time with Jesus. In just a few minutes, he changed her life forever. She wondered, "Can this be the Christ?" Who else could have known her life so completely, and who else could offer her eternal life?

What would it mean for Christ to transform your life? What would it mean for you to grow into a godly woman? Will Christ be your all in all? Will he be the true center of your life?

PART 2:

Am I Dating the Wrong Guy?

Some men will do everything in their power to woo, charm, amaze, cajole, manipulate, and win your affections. They sell themselves as a decent bill of goods—as the right kind of guy to marry. But if you find yourself with one of these men, be very careful. Apart from genuine repentance, faith, and humility, these men are not worthy of your time.

Our goal in this section is to hear stories, to think and pray about these important matters, and to bring God's perspective to your dating relationships. My friend Charlotte looked at this section and said to me, "I think at one point or another, I've dated each of these guys." Maybe that's you, too. Think biblically, wisely, lovingly, patiently, and with Christ-likeness, and you'll begin to see why it's unwise to marry these ten kinds of men.

5

The Control Freak

Real love is incompatible
with a domineering approach to relationships.

"You know that those who are considered rulers of the
Gentiles lord it over them, and their great ones exercise
authority over them. But it shall not be so among you. But
whoever would be great among you must be your servant,
and whoever would be first among you must be slave of all.
For even the Son of Man came not to be served but to serve,
and to give his life as a ransom for many." (Mark 10:41–42)

Christian men are not characterized by control
or (to use biblical terminology) "lording over" their wife,
but by gracious, loving, servant-hearted leadership.

A husband and wife are speaking to each other.

> W: I am struggling with our new church.
> H [with a high-pitched voice]: *What? Why don't you like it?* We've
> been there for a few months now and taken a lot of time to
> find a decent church. You're not going to insist that we start
> over, are you?

Let's try this conversation again.

> W: I am struggling with our new church.
> H [with a calm tone]: Talk to me. Tell me what you are strug-
> gling with. . .

These are two very different responses. The first is a stronger reaction, where the husband argues with his wife. In the second response, he invites her to explain what she is thinking. He seeks to understand her.

A Christian man's treatment of his girlfriend or wife—whether he is loving, caring, gracious, and humble, or is instead argumentative, controlling, and manipulative—is the subject of this chapter. What does God expect from a Christian boyfriend or husband? What does biblical male leadership look like in dating and marriage? What kind of distortions should a woman be wary of? The warning of this chapter is to not marry a control freak, a man who defines manhood as ruling his wife or acts as if being "in charge" is really all there is to being a man.

Janelle and Dominique

Growing up in a Christian home, Janelle came to know Jesus in college. She had a great deal of head knowledge, and she *thought* she loved Jesus, until she faced a season of severe sickness that put her flat on her back for several months. She attended church all of her life, and even studied her Bible, but it wasn't until her health and happiness were stripped away that she came to understand what she was truly worshipping. In a period of weeks when she was bedridden and stuck at home, sleeping for hours on end, with no energy to face life, she entered into a deep depression. It was with the rescuing words of Psalm 20, "Some trust in chariots and some in horses, but we trust in the name of the LORD our God" (v. 7) that she realized that her desire for comfort and an easy life had taken over her heart. As her illness stripped these things away, she faced the painful reality—"What am I worshipping? Do I *really* love Jesus?" Her simple, honest answer at that time: "No." In the midst of the pain, however, she turned her life over to Christ. His words echoed in her heart: "Come to me, all you who are weary and burdened, and I will give you rest" (Matthew 11:28 NIV). From that day forward, Janelle was never the same. Christ mattered more to her than everything else.

Dominique followed a different path. As he was exiting the train station one day, a man stopped him and asked if he knew where he would go if he died today. Appalled by the question, Dominique ignored the man and walked on. But in that brief interaction, a seed was planted in his soul, and it was something he couldn't shake. In the days ahead, as he faced the unrest of life, and the instability of a post-9-11 terrorist world, he couldn't shake the thought of death. So, when a friend invited him to come to an Easter service, he immediately said, "yes."

The pastor preached that our rebellion against God deserves hell, but that Christ died for our sins and rose again on the third day. He shared that the assurance of what happens in the next life comes by believing in who Jesus is and what he accomplished on the cross. That's what Dominique did—he put his trust in Christ. Nothing in his life changed right away. In fact, many of his old habits stayed the same. But he continued to go to church with his friend, and picked up a Bible at a local bookstore.

Janelle and Dominique met each other while serving in the nursery at church. They chatted briefly, although neither thought much about their interaction. But they continued to run into each other, and eventually started having longer and longer conversations. Dominique asked her out. They went out a few times, enjoyed one another, and started an official dating relationship.

It was a few months into the relationship when Janelle noticed Dominique's controlling patterns. Whenever she was out with a girlfriend, he would call and ask, "Where are you?" Throughout the day, he would check in with her multiple times. At first she rationalized it—in most of her previous dating relationships, if she and her boyfriend were "into" each other, they would talk multiple times a day, so this was nothing new. However, after a period of time, Janelle had to admit something was different about Dominique's behavior. It was like he was tracking her every move, wanting to know who she was with and what she was doing at all times. She wanted to rationalize his behavior. "He's protective of me," she told herself.

A little while later, he was waiting in her living room as she finished getting ready for a date. She came out, dressed up and ready to go.

"What do you think?" she said, posing for him, hands on her hips, a huge smile on her face, waiting for his response.

"Stunning, as always, honey. But you know that blue dress you wore on our first date? I'd like you to go back and change into that . . ."

"But, I like this dress . . ."

He shot back, "Just do what I ask, okay?" She could see the flash of anger in his face. Whenever he got angry, it was sudden and out of nowhere.

She thought about arguing with him, but she knew it never helped. If she pushed back, the conversation would quickly escalate or explode. So she nodded her head ever so slightly. She quickly threw on a fake smile, turned, and headed back into her bedroom.

Over time his attempts to control her became more intense. He didn't like it when she hung out with her girlfriends. He was jealous—he often accused her of looking at other men when they were out shopping. And his criticisms of her—regarding her weight, clothing, and family—became far too common.

King of the Universe

There is a kind of man who has a twisted vision of masculinity and leadership in a relationship. Much like a boy who controls every move of his remote control car, so also these men think it is their responsibility to control the woman they are dating or the wife they marry. That's their definition of manhood—"I'm in charge. And you listen to me." The sad thing is that they believe they are doing the right thing, when in fact, they are doing irreparable harm to the relationship.

What might this controlling behavior look like? It could be keeping track of their girlfriend—calling, texting, emailing to see who she is with and what she is doing. He might check her email or texts, having no regard for her privacy. This could carry over into demands about the way a dishwasher needs to be loaded, or how the home is arranged. A controlling man gets frustrated with his wife if she doesn't do exactly as he asked. He may tell her what to wear on certain days. He gets to decide what they do, including where they go on vacation together, or who they spend time with. He finds more and more ways to exert control over her life. He is not a boyfriend or a husband; he is more like a dictator who doesn't have a country to rule, so he takes out his demands on his girlfriend or wife. He's always in charge; she must listen to him, or else he makes her life miserable by verbally berating her. Intimidation (and sometimes even physical abuse) pressures her into living under his tyranny. If she disagrees or fights back, he tries to exert greater and greater control. He's always right; she's always wrong. Over time, she doubts herself, because he consistently disregards her opinion. He's prideful; she's insecure, so he manipulates her. He's always got the higher ground in a disagreement.

This kind of behavior is wrong on so many levels, but biblically speaking, let's define why this is an affront to what true biblical manhood and womanhood should look like.

First, consider that *a wife or girlfriend has inherent value because she is an image-bearer made in the likeness of God* (Genesis 1:26–28). Though she does not physically look like God (for God is spirit, not fleshly like us), she displays a likeness to God in his moral and relational attributes—love, truthfulness, goodness, kindness, patience, mercy, and many more. There is a dignity and respect that she deserves from him simply because she is made in the likeness of God.

Second, as an image-bearer, she is not anyone's robot, but she has a spirit, a brain, emotions, and a will—all of which give her *a fundamental ability to make volitional choices on her own*. She can choose responsibly for herself. She doesn't need a boyfriend or husband to tell her what to do with every decision in her life. This doesn't eliminate the biblical criteria for a husband to lead his wife, but biblical male leadership does not command a wife in every aspect of her life; it is graciously and lovingly leading her through life, giving her direction in some things, but entrusting to her many other things without micromanaging her.

The apostle Paul writes, "And we have confidence in the Lord about you, that you are doing and will do the things that we command. May the Lord direct your hearts to the love of God and to the steadfastness of Christ" (2 Thessalonians 3:4–5). Paul trusted the Spirit of God at work in the Thessalonian Christians. Paul didn't say, "We have confidence in you," but "We have confidence in the Lord about you, that you are doing and will do the things that we command." Insecurity and fear makes a man feel like he needs to control his girlfriend or wife. A man who trusts God can trust the Spirit of God at work in his girlfriend or wife. He has no need to control.

Third, *Christian male leadership is not characterized by control or (to use biblical terminology) "lording over" someone, but by loving, servant-hearted leadership.* Jesus gives a warning and sets an example.

> And when the ten heard it, they began to be indignant at James and John. And Jesus called them to him and said to them, "You know that those who are considered rulers of the Gentiles lord it over them, and their great ones exercise authority over them. But it shall not be so among you. But whoever would be great among you must be your servant, and whoever would be first among you must be slave of all. For even the Son of Man came not to be served but to serve, and to give his life as a ransom for many." (Mark 10:41–45)

The disciples James and John once asked Jesus for a special place of honor at his right hand or left when he rules in glory (vv. 35–37). This created tension among the disciples—the other ten became "indignant" at

James and John, perhaps because of their own ambition (v. 41). Jesus gave them a warning to not lead like the secular rulers of their day, who misused their authority to control and manipulate those under them. "Don't be like them," Christ admonished, "rather, look at what I will do."

Jesus gave his life as a ransom for many. He atoned for our sins, and in so doing, he served us by giving up his life on our behalf. Rather than coming to earth to be served, which Jesus could have done as the great creator and ruler of the universe, he came to serve. Christian leadership is distinguished by following Christ's example—not to be served, but to serve (v. 45). If a Christian boyfriend or husband wants to be distinctly Christian in his leadership style, he must serve his girlfriend or wife. To do anything less is an affront to the gospel and everything that Christ did on the cross for us.

The apostle Paul articulated the same idea when he said, "Husbands, love your wives, as Christ loved the church and gave himself up for her" (Ephesians 5:25). Just as Christ loved his bride, the church, by giving up his life for her, so also a husband should love his wife in the same way. This is an analogy, where the husband is called on to live like Christ. He can't atone for sins like Christ did, but he can live a self-denying, self-sacrificial life for the sake of his wife, which is what the Lord requires of him. This is the true nature of a biblical husband's role.

Some men falsely import military or corporate concepts of leadership into a Christian relationship between a husband and wife. The man thinks that leading means acting like a general commanding a sergeant or a CEO ordering an employee—a hierarchy where he is in charge. Instead, biblically speaking, picture a husband, holding his wife's hand, and lovingly leading her forward, hand-in-hand, facing life together. Throw out the idea of a general barking orders at his subordinates or a CEO dictating tasks to his employees. A Christian man lovingly, sacrificially, thoughtfully, graciously, and carefully walks forward with his wife.

Fourth and finally, *a humble and wise man knows who is truly sovereign—God—and not himself.* Any man who feels the need for control has lost sight of who is really in charge of the universe. God is in charge. Consider the Lord's own words from the book of Isaiah:

> Do you not know? Do you not hear? Has it not been told you from the beginning? Have you not understood from the foundations of the earth? It is he who sits above the circle of the earth, and its inhabitants are like grasshoppers; who stretches out the

heavens like a curtain, and spreads them like a tent to dwell in; who brings princes to nothing, and makes the rulers of the earth as emptiness. (Isaiah 40:21–23)

God is in charge. He marks off the heavens and stretches them out like his very own tent (v. 22). Rulers of the world are like grasshoppers to him, and he commands when they rise and when they fall (v. 23). He creates every star, brings them out, names each one, and ensures none are missing (v. 26). God is sovereign over every stretch of this world and every person who dwells in it.

A Christian man should live in a way that shows who is truly sovereign in his life and in the lives of those around him. For example, the Christian man shows his dependence on God by daily turning to him in prayer (1 Thessalonians 5:17). Asking God for help shows that he knows who is really in charge. In stark contrast, a man who manipulates and controls a woman—through his words, sex, flirtation, threats, withdrawal, or passive-aggressive games—is not trusting in God's sovereignty, but instead is taking matters into his own hands. Fundamentally, this man's need to be in control shows his lack of trust in God.

Divorce Predictions: Husbands Who Refuse to Be Influenced by Their Wives

A man who demands control gives his girlfriend or wife very little opportunity for input into their marriage or into life in general. Best-selling author and marriage researcher John Gottman says that husbands who refuse to be influenced by their wives end up divorced. Based on this idea, in a longitudinal study of 130 newlywed couples he found that with about 80% accuracy, he could predict which couples would end up no longer married.[1]

Contrast the two following conversations.[2] In the first, the wife makes a simple request for her husband to get along better with her mother:

> W: I know my mom can be hard to be around, but could you make an effort to spend some time talking to her?
> H: (Sarcastically) So, what do you want anyway? You want me to just be agreeable all the time, do what you want, do what your mother wants?

Accepting influence means finding something agreeable with the wife's request. In Christian marriage, the husband learns from and listens to his wife. He moves toward her in a conversation rather than away from her. Even if he doesn't agree, he's willing to listen and consider her request. A distinctly Christian marriage requires humility and a servant-like attitude on the husband's part. In the example above, the husband is harsh in his response and unwilling to listen to his wife or to make any kind of compromise.

In a second example, the wife asks her husband to make a change.

> W: It would really help me if you could work from home one day a week. What do you think?
>
> H: Fine by me. Right now, I have enough stuff to do I could easily work at home.

What a stark contrast. While the interaction was brief, the husband saw that his wife's request was reasonable and was willing to accept her desires as something good for both of them. He was willing to be influenced by her because he was eager for them to find common ground. He listened to her, humbly received her request, and even quickly agreed with her. He recognized her as a gift from God to help him. Therefore, he gladly received her suggestion.

Don't equate a husband accepting influence as a wife's opportunity to be in charge of the marriage; it shouldn't be that a husband agrees simply to keep the peace in the family or because he is too passive to lead his wife. A husband accepting influence from his wife is never an excuse for the husband to give up his leadership role in the marriage. In the end, the husband is responsible before God first and foremost for the welfare of his family. *However, a loving, humble, servant-hearted, and gracious Christian husband will listen to his wife, consider her requests, and fight for unity in their decision-making.* Even when he doesn't agree, he listens to her, understands her and builds bridges with her, all the while never giving up his leadership role in the marriage. He does this to honor God, to care for his wife, and to build a healthy, unified marriage, for the good of his family.

Why Did Janelle Settle?

Janelle settled for Dominique because she devalued her life as a single adult. She had a poor understanding of the beauty and value of singleness. She felt like folks in church looked down on her as a single adult, and in general she felt inferior to married couples. Believing that marriage was somehow a superior way to live, she thought, *Let me just get married, then*

I can work all these other things out. She struggled with fears of loneliness, discontentment with her singleness, insecurity about herself, and frustrations with her life in general. So she rationalized, "If my circumstances change (regardless of the person I marry), my life will immediately get better. I won't be lonely anymore; I'll have a man to rely on, and I'll be more happy." She wasn't ignorant to the fact that Dominique was controlling, but she was more focused on the painful realities of her singleness. The grass was greener on the other side. The tradeoff was worth it to her.

Paired with this, she wrongly overestimated what the change of circumstances in marriage might bring. She believed, "I won't be as lonely anymore," yet she didn't realize that a lot of married people are very lonely. Marriage is not a paradise. As one pastor commented, "Being single and lonely is better than being married and lonely."

She also believed, "I can change him." She overestimated her ability to influence him. She assumed he would listen to her in marriage, even though he didn't listen to her in their dating relationship. She married with an eye toward the man she wanted him to be, not the man he was right then.

Piled on top of all of her other fears—loneliness, never having children, being unmarried for the rest of her life—was the fear of missing out. Missing out on what all her friends had (marriage, children, a man, a home, a fulfilling life). Missing out on special memories (her wedding day, children, and growing old together). Missing out on moments of intimacy. Missing out on what the church values when it comes to evaluating maturity (Married people are more mature than single people, right? Married people always talk about how marriage helps you with your selfishness).

Because Janelle is insecure about herself, she often thinks, *Maybe I deserve the way he treats me.* She's always questioned herself, wondering if anyone would ever love her, and fearing that she wasn't good enough for a husband. Because she thought so poorly of herself, it was not hard to accept Dominique. "I know this guy has got problems, but who else is going to love me?" She didn't expect the good guys—the really godly men at church—to ever pay attention to her.

Janelle knew that her relationship had problems and that the guy she was dating didn't meet the biblical criteria of a loving husband, but she didn't want to have to start over. She thought, *This guy knows me, we are making it work, he's fun, and I like him.* It just seemed like too much work to untangle the relationship and start over again. Wrapped up in that was her own fear of exposure—"If I admit that this guy isn't it, then I've got to admit (again) that a relationship isn't working out, and I just don't want to do that." Maybe Janelle's pride was getting in the way? She wasn't humble enough to admit her wrong choice in a guy when her friends pointed out Dominique's controlling behavior. She made excuses for him, but she knew the truth. She didn't want to find another guy and start the dating process all over again. It was just too painful.

Think for a moment about yourself—are you at all like Janelle? Do you think so poorly of yourself that you'd be willing to settle for a problematic relationship? Perhaps you too ignore important issues because your fears are too big, and God is too small. Are you confident you can change the guy, regardless of how much he doesn't love God or live like a Christian man? It's easy to believe that the grass is always greener on the other side, and that marriage just has to be better than your current life.

Ditch a Controlling Man

A controlling man can use the Bible to get his girlfriend or wife to do what he wants. He might proclaim, "The Bible says the man is in charge," or "God says you should submit to me!" or "The Lord is telling me . . ." or "Just trust and obey; stop worrying so much." He uses the Bible to manipulate her and to feed his selfishness. He lords it over her through spiritual language that is twisted to support his demands.

Maybe the guy's control comes in a form that is less spiritualized—he is just overbearing in his demands, jealousies, or insecurities. Maybe he has an overbearing personality, and he knows how to manipulate a woman with deep insecurities.

Maybe he is a demanding micromanager at work, so he runs his home just like he does his job. He's a dictator in his own home.

As hard as it is to believe, these guys can change with growing maturity, but it's best to not date them until they do. Don't assume, like Janelle, that you can change the guy. Better to break it off with a controlling man, and not marry him, than to face a lifetime of treatment as an inferior person. No one deserves this. God doesn't treat us this way. If God is loving, gracious, and merciful—why would you ever think to settle for anything less than a kind, thoughtful, Christ-centered man?

6
The Promiscuous Guy

One of Satan's most effective strategies to corrupt the gospel-portraying union of marriage is to attack couples through sexual sin before they say "I do." – Garrett Kell[1]

For this is the will of God, your sanctification: that you abstain from sexual immorality; that each one of you know how to control his own body in holiness and honor, not in the passion of lust like the Gentiles who do not know God; that no one transgress and wrong his brother in this matter, because the Lord is an avenger in all these things, as we told you beforehand and solemnly warned you. For God has not called us for impurity, but in holiness. Therefore whoever disregards this, disregards not man but God, who gives his Holy Spirit to you. (1 Thessalonians 4:3–8)

Sex is a powerful means that God uses to build unity between a man and a woman.

As a brand-new pastor, one of my first surprises was the responses I received to a question on our premarital inventory: "Do you sometimes feel guilty about sexual involvement you have had with your fiancé?" I knew that unbelievers eagerly pursued sex. The sexual revolution of the 1960s and '70s made the personal pursuit of sex a glorious ideal. Today sex is flaunted, sold, talked about, exalted, and prized. Our culture loves to pursue sex, and has no shame in it. No more hiding behind closed doors. But Christians? Don't they have God's Word and the power of the Holy Spirit? Shouldn't they look different than the world? But as I read through the responses, I was surprised by how often Christians struggle with premarital sex, pornography, masturbation, wandering eyes, flirtatious behavior, and everything that goes along with this. All too often the answer to the question, "Do you sometimes feel guilty?" was "Yes!"

It shouldn't surprise you then that I've included a chapter asking you to not date or marry a promiscuous guy. Whether it is due to their own desires, or something they feel they have to do in order to secure the relationship, or even because they don't understand God's design for our sexuality (or a combination of all of these things), too many Christian women get drawn into and willingly participate in sex before marriage. Premarital sex does great harm to their consciences and to their relationship with Christ. Consider one woman's story as she came to terms with this sin in her own life.

Thomas and Samantha

Thomas and Samantha had been dating for just a few days, when he reached out to hold her hand. She smiled. This was the first time he showed physical affection.

Over the next few months, the affection grew. A hand on her back. Sitting side-by-side, bodies touching. Kiss on the cheek. A kiss on the lips. Snuggling while watching a movie on the couch. A longer, deeper kiss. It progressed over a few weeks to full make-out sessions—heated and passionate. His hands drifted, touching different parts of her body. They'd rub up against each other. Eventually clothes came off and they consummated the relationship.

Every time it happened, she felt guilty. They'd talk about it afterwards, maybe that day, or the next day. Samantha would cry. Thomas would apologize. And yet, the very next time they were together, it happened again.

Samantha was a virgin prior to meeting Thomas. Sex was exciting, and it felt good, but she suffered under the weight of her guilt. She grew up in a Christian home and made a profession of faith in college. She studied her Bible, went to church, and had a close circle of Christian friends. When Thomas came along and initiated the relationship, she responded because no one else had ever asked her out. He seemed like a responsible and kind guy, and well liked by many folks in the church.

Thomas was in the military. He was tall, clean-cut, and hard working. He prayed a prayer in high school after a friend told him about Jesus. With his military job, he moved around from city to city every few years, so he never grew deep relationships in a church. He did read his Bible, but he didn't get much out of it. He struggled with lust, and dated quite a bit, which was dangerous because it often led to premarital sex. His father told him things like, "Women are put on earth to give us pleasure." Thomas knew that was wrong, but that's essentially how he treated women too. The goal of a dating relationship was to satisfy his lust. He'd always lead a girlfriend in the direction of more intimacy, and if the girl put up a protest, he'd put pressure on her until she gave in. He approached every relationship as if it was a conquest and several girls lost their virginity to Thomas.

God's Purposes for Sex

God has three purposes for sex. Here they are, but not necessarily in order of importance! The first is *for making babies*. God commands men and women from the very beginning, in the creation account, to have children. In Genesis 1:28, Scripture tells us, "God blessed them and said to them, 'Be fruitful and increase in number; fill the earth and subdue it.'" The fruit of physical intimacy is pregnancy and bearing children. Whether you like it or not, this is how God designed it. If you want to have sex, you need to be ready for children.

The second purpose is what most people assume—sex is *for pleasure*. Song of Solomon describes the satisfaction that comes in being intimate with his loved one. The beloved declares: "My lover is to me a sachet of myrrh resting between my breasts" (1:13) and "My lover is mine and I am his; he browses among the lilies" (2:16). We see the delight that comes from partaking in physical love with your spouse. The beloved proclaims, "Let him kiss me with the kisses of his mouth— for your love is more delightful than wine" (1:2). The lover, in viewing his beloved bride, comments in response,

> "How delightful is your love, my sister, my bride! How much more pleasing is your love than wine, and the fragrance of your perfume than any spice! Your lips drop sweetness as the honeycomb, my bride; milk and honey are under your tongue. The fragrance of your garments is like that of Lebanon" (4:11–12).

People have sex because they enjoy it; they like the pleasure that comes from being intimate with their spouse. Many pursue pleasure out of selfish motives—for their personal enjoyment. For them, sex is never anything more than what they can get out of it. But for the Christian, sex is more. It's something God gives us for our joy.

Most people associate sex with these first two purposes; yet, there is more to sex than just procreation and pleasure. The third purpose for sex is *to bring unity to a husband and wife*. God uses intimacy to build unity between a man and a woman. Sex is the most vulnerable of acts you can ever partake in. You take off your clothes, expose yourself to someone, and give over your body. The world reduces sex to the selfish pursuit of pleasure—so trust, love, and commitment are thrown out, and you can literally hook-up with anyone anywhere so long as you both consent to it. A Christian vantage point on sex is radically different. Sex is best when it is given to someone you trust; someone to whom you are committed for life. Trust, commitment, and sex are meant to go hand-in-hand. Being vulnerable with someone you don't trust (or have not consented to) is *a nightmare*. That's one reason why rape is so evil. Being vulnerable with someone you trust and are committed to is *wonderful*. God uses this combination of vulnerability, pleasure, and trust to build unity between a man and a woman. Most people pursue sex for personal pleasure alone, but God intends through sex to give so much more.

An obvious question comes next: "This sounds wonderful, so can anyone have this?" No, God says sex belongs in marriage. It's a gift to a man and a woman who have committed themselves to each other. Trust, commitment, and sex go hand-in-hand with marriage. The Bible explains this *positively*—when married, a man and woman are "one flesh" or "one" (Genesis 2:24; Mark 10:5–9), which means they are united relationally, financially, emotionally, spiritually, and of course, physically. A husband and wife are to give themselves to each other sexually (1 Corinthians 7:1–5). *Negatively*, the Bible warns against any kind of sexual immorality (Mark 7:21; Acts 15:20; Romans 13:13; 1 Corinthians 5:11; 6:15, 18; 7:2; 10:8; Galatians 5:19), and speaks out against premarital and extramarital sex (Proverbs 5—7; Matthew 5:28; Ephesians 5:3; 1 Thessalonians 4:3–8). The marriage bed must be kept pure because God will judge adulterers and immoral people (Hebrews 13:4).

These are God's intentions as he gives men and women this wonderful gift of sexual intimacy. He designed sex for our pleasure and for bearing children. So also, he gives men and women in marriage the gift of sex for their enjoyment and for his glory.

Singleness and Sex

The skeptic says, "Really? Seriously?" Today's culture exalts sex. Everyone partakes. Christians are prudish and Puritans if they refrain.

Plenty of single Christians give in to cultural pressures and give in to their own lustful desires. They exercise little control over their bodies. And no one holds them accountable.

Consider Paul's exhortation in Romans 13:12–14.

> The night is far gone; the day is at hand. . . . Let us walk properly as in the daytime, not in orgies and drunkenness, not in sexual immorality and sensuality, not in quarreling and jealousy. But put on the Lord Jesus Christ, and make no provision for the flesh, to gratify its desires.

In light of Christ returning (v. 12 "the day is at hand"), the Christian is to be thoughtful about how she behaves. She should not partake in drinking, partying, sexual immorality, and fighting (v. 13). She is to clothe herself in Christ (v. 14), adopting a new way of life reflective of the fruits of the Spirit. She is to not do anything that aides the sinful nature and satisfies its desires (v. 14). If you are having sex outside of marriage, you are satisfying your own selfish, lustful desires. Every time you think about sex, plan for it, welcome it, or allow it, you make "provision for the flesh." And as you gratify your sexual desires, it craves for more. It is never satisfied; it always wants more. Remember our discussion about the woman at the well who encountered Jesus (John 4:1–42) in chapter 4? She had five different husbands, and none of them satisfied her desires. It was only when she met Christ that she found real satisfaction. So also, your own desires will never be satisfied apart from Christ.

Consider also 1 Thessalonians 4:3–8 where Paul describes God's will for our lives.

> For this is the will of God, your sanctification: that you abstain from sexual immorality; that each one of you know how to control his own body in holiness and honor, not in the passion of lust like the Gentiles who do not know God; that no one transgress and wrong his brother in this matter, because the Lord is an avenger in all these things, as we told you beforehand and solemnly warned you. For God has not called us for impurity, but in holiness. Therefore whoever disregards this, disregards not man but God, who gives his Holy Spirit to you.

This is another passage in which Paul is instructing the Christians in how they are to live in order to please God (v. 1). The word "sanctification" can also be translated "holiness." Holiness is a chief concern of Paul's (vv. 3, 4, 7, 8). To be holy is to be set apart from sin. Just as the nation of Israel was to be holy—set apart from the sins of the other nations (Exodus 19:5–6; Leviticus 20:23–26), so also Paul is calling Christians to holy living.[2]

It is God's will that Christians should be sexually pure (1 Thessalonians 4:3). They should refrain from sexual immorality in any form (premarital or extramarital). They are to be self-controlled with their bodies, restraining their passionate lust (vv. 4–5; cf. 1 Corinthians 7:1–9). The pagans, who did not know God, indulged in sexual revelry, and Christians were to be distinct from them (v. 5; cf. Romans 1). Paul describes in verse 6: "that no one transgress and *wrong* his brother in this matter." Another translation (NASB) puts it more sharply: "that no man transgress and *defraud* his brother." To defraud is to cheat someone; taking something that belongs to another. When you have premarital or extramarital sex, you cheat the other person by taking something that doesn't belong to you. You are quite literally robbing from them. And if he or she ends up getting married one day, you also cheat his or her future spouse by taking what should only belong to them (1 Corinthians 7:2–3). You are stealing from someone else's marriage. Be warned: God will punish all those who commit such sins (v. 6). If you don't like this, or are tempted to disregard it because you don't want to give up sex, don't argue with me, argue with God (v. 8). He calls us not to be impure, but to make holiness our goal (v. 7).

Consider a third text: 1 Timothy 5:1–2.

> Do not rebuke an older man but encourage him as you would a father, younger men as brothers, older women as mothers, younger women as sisters, in all purity.

In the Bible, there are only three kinds of relationships that a man can have with a woman—either she is his biological mother or sister, his spiritual mother or sister in Christ, or she is his wife. So when Paul addresses Timothy, how does he expect Timothy to treat the younger women in the church? "As sisters, in all purity" (v. 2). First and foremost, a man should treat a single woman as a sister in Christ. Just as incest (a brother sexualizing his relationship with his sister) is wrong, so also a single man should not sexualize his relationship with a woman. God's standard is for the single man to treat every single woman in "absolute" purity (NIV, v. 2). Remember, sexual holiness is the goal.

Now at this point, some of you are thinking, *Okay, I get it. Stop beating a dead horse. Why keep reading passage after passage that says the same thing? Sexual immorality is wrong.* Consider two things.[3]

First, this is more than just saying no to sex, no to making provisions for the flesh, and no to defrauding. Holiness and honor is the goal. Purity is hard in an oversexualized culture that says, "Take, take, take!" or "There is nothing wrong with this!" or "God's standards are archaic." Yet, this is *God's* standard—absolute purity. He says, "Be holy as I am holy" (1 Peter 1:16). Anything less than this is dishonoring to God.

Second, it's important to feel the weight of Scripture, passage after passage. Because our flesh craves sex and our selfish desires are powerful, Christians are often tempted to disobey. We need God's standard to ring loudly in our ears because the voice in us and the voices around us want nothing more than for us to abandon God's Word. Therein is the fight—will you listen to your sinful desires and the culture, or will you listen to God?

Why Did Samantha Settle?

Samantha settled for Thomas because she was tempted to believe lies, like "Men won't stay if you don't give them sex," or "You've got to give a man what he wants, or else he'll find another woman who will give it to him." As crude as this sounds, Christian women buy into this junk, and they let these lies dictate how they handle their dating relationships.

Samantha also settled because she lost her virginity to Thomas, so she felt like she *had* to marry him. Sure, love was a part of it, but obligation was an even bigger part. After all, she had saved herself for one man. She slept with Thomas, so he must be *that* man. If she let him go, she would be the equivalent of a slut, giving herself to guys (plural), not just one guy.

Finally, she settled because she felt guilty. Sex was beautiful, but it was also powerful. Though Thomas often initiated, she reciprocated. She wanted it just as much as he did. She didn't heed Solomon's warning: "Do not arouse or awaken love until it so desires" (Song of Solomon 2:7 NIV). She felt complicit in the sexual relationship.

For the Guilty and Ashamed

What if this is you? What if you, like Samantha, feel guilty for your sexual immorality? You know you are wrong, but you feel powerless to change yourself or your relationship. There are a few things that are important for you to hear.[4]

In Christ, you are forgiven. If you repent of your sins and trust in Christ, his blood washes away your sin. Don't walk around like a white sheep with black spots. That's what many Christians are like—they walk around consistently feeling guilty for past sexual transgressions. No, your soul is whiter than snow (Psalm 51:7). It might sound too good to be true, but believe it. Christ has "freed us from our sins by his blood" (Revelation 1:5). Don't let guilt and shame weigh down your soul. Go to Jesus and ask for forgiveness and help. Start with a simple prayer, "Lord Jesus, show mercy to me."

Don't be passive; flee sexual immorality. If you are fighting for purity, don't be passive about this sin. Jesus encourages us to take radical steps to fight our sin:

> "If your right eye causes you to sin, tear it out and throw it away. For it is better that you lose one of your members than that your whole body be thrown into hell. And if your right hand causes you to sin, cut it off and throw it away. For it is better that you lose one of your members than that your whole body go into hell." (Matthew 5:29–30)

He doesn't want you to literally cut off your hand or gouge out your eye. But he uses hyperbole—exaggeration—to make the point. Don't be passive about sin; take drastic measures to get rid of it. What would that mean for you? What does fleeing look like? Does it mean you need to break up with the guy, if he won't stop initiating sex? Does it mean you need to get accountability—confessing your sin to God and other believers? Does it mean you need to get back into the Word, pray again, and get back into church? Does it mean changing the way you dress, talk, and act? These are questions you can ask the Lord and others to help you sort through. Paul's consistent exhortation is to flee sexual immorality (1 Corinthians 6:18; 2 Timothy 2:22). Don't be passive, but run (as fast as you can) in the opposite direction.

Find accountability. If you are not in a local church, then go to one this Sunday and ask the pastor to connect you with a godly older woman who can help you sort through your situation. Pride (and possibly fear of being exposed) makes us want to try to fight this battle on our own, but we can't. God's design is for us to get help. We need others to help us battle these sexual sins and encourage us to fight for faith. Get accountability quickly. Open up your life and be vulnerable and honest about your sin. Encourage your accountability partner to ask blunt, intrusive, and honest questions. Be willing to put to death your pride. Be quick to confess sin. And don't short-circuit your accountability by *only* talking about your sexual sin. There are layers of reasons why you were involved in sexual intimacy before marriage, so talk about fighting sin, but also uncover together some of the deeper reasons you were sexually involved, then read the Bible, pray together, and sort through what it means to live for Christ.

Finally, submit to Christ's lordship. To reduce this conversation to a fleshly battle of fighting sexual temptation loses sight of the most important of ingredients—faith in Christ. As you come to terms with what I've said in this chapter, ask yourself: Do I trust and believe God, and am I willing to align my life with how he has designed me, marriage, and sexual intimacy, or do I want to do things my own way and follow what the rest of the world is doing? Putting all of your faith in Christ means choosing to follow God in everything.

How Premarital Sex Affects Marriage

Many Christians don't think about the harm that premarital sex can do to a future marriage. Consider two things.

Just because God gives you freedom to have sex in marriage doesn't mean everything will be perfect after you tie the knot. Trust issues can emerge. Doubt can arise in the wife's mind. She thinks, *He couldn't control himself before marriage, how am I supposed to trust him at work with other women?* Premarital sex establishes a pattern where the wife doubts the husband's integrity. And no surprise—the seeds of doubt start in dating, but they can grow in marriage, especially as they experience stress.

Also, because the couple let their desires lead before marriage, those same selfish desires (James 4:1–3) continue to lead in marriage. If you were both selfish in your pursuit of sex before marriage, that pattern can easily continue. If you build your life around your selfish desires, it will ruin your marriage.

Ditch the Promiscuous Guy

Sexual promiscuity is all-too-common in our day, even among Christians. It might seem impossible to find a man who cares more about purity and holiness, but that's God's standard, so make it your standard too. Don't date or marry the promiscuous guy. He's not worthy of your time.

7

The Unchurched Guy

A person who is half-hearted about the church is half-hearted about Christ. We can't claim to love Christ and be lackadaisical about His bride, the church. It's not possible. If we feel like we can take or leave the church, we must realize we risk losing Christ.
– Candice Watters[1]

His intent was that now, through the church, the manifold wisdom of God should be made known to the rulers and authorities in the heavenly realms, according to his eternal purpose that he accomplished in Christ Jesus our Lord.
(Ephesians 3:10–11 NIV)

Your best plan for spiritual growth is to stay connected to Christians assembled in a local church in your community.

"Church matters."

I remember the first time someone said this to me. Even though I have been a church-goer for most of my life, for many of those years, I confess that I didn't understand why church *should* matter to me. I just knew it was something my parents taught me to do—go to church regularly.

But why? Is it enough to go to church because my parents taught me to do it? Maybe your reason is not the same as mine. Why do you go to church? Does it help you be more religious? Is it a good place to meet other people or find a spouse? Will it help you be a better person? Just think about this for a moment—does church really matter *to you*? How does your life show that it really does matter to you? Should church matter when it comes to dating and marriage? If so, how?

We need to explore the role of church in your life and in your dating life. Church should matter to you. And it should matter to anyone you date. The question is—why?

Danny and Jamika

Jamika worked as an accountant for a large firm. She liked her job, and she was good at it.

Danny was in the same office and he would often stop by Jamika's desk to talk with her. Casual conversations turned into longer conversations. Jamika often thought, *He must be interested, otherwise he wouldn't be paying so much attention to me.*

Jamika was a Christian. Her parents were not religious, but her grandmother often brought her to church. In high school, she lied to her parents and got into all sorts of trouble, but underneath her tough exterior was a girl who dreaded failure. Her life changed after hearing the pastor teach on 1 Corinthians 1:27–29 (NIV): "But God chose the foolish things in the world to shame the wise; God chose the weak things in the world to shame the strong; God chose the lowly and despised things—the things that are not—to nullify the things that are, so that no one may boast before him." Jesus turned her world upside down. She emerged from that sermon with a deep hunger to know God's Word, and her life was transformed overnight. Even her parents were surprised at the sudden changes in her life—her submission to their authority, honesty, and cheerful spirit.

As Jamika grew in her friendship with Danny, she was initially guarded. Most of her previous dating relationships had not gone well. With time, Danny's consistent attention, politeness, and kindness toward her kept her open to him. A few weeks later, after stopping by for a quick chat, Danny noticed a Bible on her desk.

"Are you religious?"

"Yes, I'm a Christian."

"I could tell . . . you never curse and you don't sleep around."

"Well, I guess that was a compliment?" A smile glistened on her face. Danny never beat around the bush. He was often direct.

Danny responded, "I'm a Christian."

Jamika's eyes widened and she quipped, "Really?"

He shot back, "Why did you say it that way?" He looked concerned.

"Well, you do curse. You are out partying almost every night of the week. But at least you are polite to me." Jamika's smile grew a little wider. "Where do you go to church?"

Danny replied, "I haven't gone to church in years."

Without any hesitation, Jamika responded, "You're welcome to join me for church. I've been going to First Baptist Church with my grandmother ever since I was a little kid. My grandmother would love to have company on a Sunday."

"Okay, maybe I will do that." Jamika couldn't tell if Danny was being polite or if he was serious.

Danny followed through. He joined Jamika and her grandmother at church the next Sunday. Encouraged by Danny's interest in church, Jamika started accepting more of Danny's invitations to spend time together.

Danny says he is a Christian and he is even open to going to church with Jamika, though his lifestyle doesn't show it and he hasn't been to church on his own for several years. Did Jamika make a good decision when she decided to start spending more time with Danny?

Building Your Life around a Local Church

Does it really matter that Danny doesn't go to church? After all, he says he is a Christian. Isn't that good enough? To answer these questions, let's consider what a church is and why it is essential for your spiritual life, and your decision about a future husband.

When you think of the word *church* you probably think of a building with a steeple on top. The actual word *church* refers to a gathering or an assembly of Christians. A church is a specific group of people who regularly gather together to worship God in one specific location. It's not a place or a building. It's a group of people committed to Christ. Think of Jesus's words, "For where two or three are gathered in my name, there am I among them" (Matthew 18:20).

Why should church be important for Danny? Consider three things.

The church is the center of God's plan for advancing his kingdom. The apostle Paul writes:

> His intent was that now, through the church, the manifold wisdom of God should be made known to the rulers and authorities in the heavenly realms, according to his eternal purpose that he accomplished in Christ Jesus our Lord. (Ephesians 3:10–11 NIV)

God's intent is that his wisdom would be made known through local churches. If this is where God displays wisdom, why wouldn't you want to be a part of it?

Have you ever noticed who is with God in the book of Revelation? There are all kinds of interesting spiritual beings—Satan thrown into the pit of fire, cherubim and angels, and the elders of Israel gathered around the throne. But at the wedding supper of the Lamb, the bride who has made herself ready, is she a girl dressed in white ready to walk down an aisle? No. The bride is *the church*. The bride is all those who have trusted in Christ and now have been gathered together to be with him (Revelation 7:9; 14:1; 19:1, 6). Marriage between a groom and a bride is used throughout Scripture as a way to describe God's covenant relationship with his church. Human marriage is a dim reflection of the greatest of all marriages—the spiritual marriage of God with his people. From the beginning to the very end of history, God has made the church central to his plan of redemption.

Christians are commanded to gather together regularly. The author of Hebrews writes, "And let us consider how to stir up one another to love and good works, not neglecting to meet together, as is the habit of some, but encouraging one another, and all the more as you see the Day drawing near" (10:24–25). Going to church is not optional. If you profess to be a Christian, regular attendance at a local church is commanded by Scripture. We should feel an obligation to gather with other Christians, and if we don't, we are wrong. But why is gathering together so important?

Your best plan for spiritual growth is to stay connected to Christians assembled in a local church in your community. In other words, build your life around a local church because you can't survive without one. A spirit of individualism makes too many of us think, "I can do this on my own. I don't need others to help." But that's just pride rearing its ugly head.

Just consider the "one another" passages in the Bible. Every Christian is obliged to love others—which includes being devoted to each other (Romans 12:10), honoring and accepting (Romans 15:17), instructing (Romans 15:14), being compassionate and quick to forgive (Ephesians 4:32), and lending courage (1 Thessalonians 5:11). A Christian needs loving, redemptive relationships in order to grow in Christ. The best place to find these kinds of relationships is a local, gospel-preaching church.

Now, after this short tour of the importance of a local church, what do you think of Danny? If he is a Christian, is it okay for him to be "unchurched"? If he abandons God's master plan (to display his wisdom through the church, Ephesians 3:10), he ignores an explicit biblical command to gather with other believers (Hebrews 10:24–25), and he puts in jeopardy his own spiritual growth (John 13:34–35; Ephesians 4:15–16), should Jamika stick with him?

Don't Settle

Lisa was in my office, having another conversation with me about singleness in the Christian life. We had had several heartfelt conversations about what it means to be content in Christ and to trust that he will be sufficient in everything.

A guy had recently expressed interest in her. They talked and spent time together. Eventually she ended the relationship. As she told me, "Church isn't important in his life, and so I figured if he is not prioritizing church, how is he going to lead *me* to prioritize church when I am his wife?"

Lisa wanted to marry a man devoted to a local church—a man who showed with his words and actions that church mattered to him. She knew that church was vital for her spiritual growth, so she wouldn't settle for a man who didn't care about church.

Does this sound crazy to you? What if the guy is kind, organized, works hard, earns a good paycheck, is kind to his mother, seems like he would make a good dad, and (most importantly for you) seems to like you? What if he hasn't gone to church in years, but calls himself a "Christian"? Am I saying that you should still say "no" to this guy? Lisa did.

You might not agree with Lisa. But that begs that question: Does church matter to you? If it doesn't matter, then you might not see anything wrong with dating Danny. That shows that you don't quite understand how important the church is to God's plan for redemption, and how important it is for you in your own personal spiritual growth. Consider a few questions below.

1. Why do you go to church? List the reasons. Is it because your parents taught you to do it? Is it for social reasons—it's a good place to meet decent people and make friends? Is it because you are lonely? Is it because you think of yourself as a Christian and you figure it is what you are supposed to do (a sense of obligation)? Is there some other reason?

2. When other things like work, school, activities, personal hobbies, or rest after a busy week demand your time, do you prioritize

these things over regular church attendance? Why do these things matter to you more than involvement in a local church?

3. Is the most important thing in your life to know Christ, to follow him, and to grow in greater love with him? If so, how are you going to accomplish that—by studying the Bible on your own? Prior to reading this chapter, did you understand the role of church in your own spiritual growth?

4. Are you going to a Bible-believing, Christ-honoring, gospel-preaching church? Find a faithful church you can be eager to attend—where the members have a clear sense that they are sinners and desperately need a Savior; where the members fight for faith and daily pursue how to earnestly love one another. Maybe your problem is that you don't go to a church that is helping you to grow spiritually. If so, find another church that is committed to explaining to you who Jesus is by faithfully teaching you from the Scriptures.

5. If you go to church, what would it take for you to get more involved in your congregation? What is holding you back?

Ask a wise, older woman of faith to talk over these questions with you. If church is not a priority, then marrying a man who is devoted to his church is just not going to make sense to you. It won't appear on your list of criteria for a good husband, even though it should.

Are Your Standards for a Boyfriend Too Low?

At this point, we can't really tell if Danny is a Christian in name only, or if he genuinely believes in Christ. If he is a believer, his faith is probably weak from not being to church in years.

Jamika has certainly set her standards too low—she is okay with a guy if he at least calls himself a Christian and is willing to come to church (at least a few times, maybe even regularly). A smart guy knows how to get a woman's attention by showing affection, attention, kindness, politeness, buying her nice things, saying sweet things, or telling her how attractive she is. He might even go to church with her and say he is "a Christian." But that doesn't mean that Danny really loves the Lord. Only time will reveal the depth of his commitment to the Lord. Jamika needs to be careful—Danny might be pursuing church because he is attracted to her.

God cares so much for us that he gave us local churches as incubators for our faith. Choose a local church, throw yourself into the daily life of that church, sit regularly under the teaching of God's Word, and submerge yourself in loving, redemptive relationships. If you love Jesus, you'll grow in greater hunger for his Word. A casual or occasional reading of the Bible won't do. Terminally superficial relationships won't do you any good either. Immerse yourself into the life of the church by building deep relationships with other Christians who can help you see, smell, taste, and understand what it means to live like Jesus. When you love God's Word and God's people, then your criteria for a boyfriend will be set with an eye toward what God wants. He wants you to love Jesus, and by natural extension, to want to be with his bride, the church. To take it one step further—if you love Jesus, and you love his bride (the church), why would you ever settle for a man who doesn't make Jesus's bride, the church, a priority?

A Sneak Peek into the Future

You might be wondering what happened with Jamika and Danny. Jamika dated Danny, and Danny went to church with Jamika while they were dating. Then they got married. In the first year of marriage, Danny stopped going to church. Jamika was surprised, but should she have been?

They probably didn't talk about spiritual things while they were dating. Apart from going to church together, he didn't ever talk about the Lord on their dates. If they talked about Christianity, it was because Jamika initiated the conversation, not him. Given his track record, it wasn't surprising that Danny didn't make spiritual matters a priority in their marriage.

How does this show up as I talk to Christian wives who married their own "Dannys"? Some of their husbands have come to church for years, but haven't built relationships with other men, or at best, have superficial relationships with other men. Their husbands don't study the Word on their own, and don't pursue spiritual conversations at home. Their husbands don't teach the children about Jesus.

Give Danny a Chance

What if Danny was repentant of his sin? What if he understood he was a sinner and was grieved over the fact that his sin was an offense against God? What if this realization drove him to the Savior? What if Danny was teachable? Maybe God would give him a humble attitude that is willing to listen to others.

If Danny was repentant and teachable, conversations with Jamika, her grandmother, and older Christian men at First Baptist Church would help him to see his need for Christ (his first priority) and also his need to be deeply involved in a local church.

Only *after* he gets his spiritual priorities in order—eagerly pursuing Jesus and getting connected with a local church—should Jamika consider Danny as a potential boyfriend. Anything sooner than this is selling herself short.

Marry a Man Committed to the Church

Lisa or Jamika? Who do you want to be? If Lisa waits patiently for a man committed to his local church, one day as a wife she won't be left to sort through life and marriage on her own. Even if Lisa and her husband go through a hard season, they won't be left alone. They'll have a vibrant community of believers who will assist them in their fight for faith in Christ. The saints will love them, care for them, pray for them, help them, grieve with them, rejoice with them, and most importantly, worship the risen Jesus with them. And that's in part because Lisa didn't sell herself short with a boyfriend who didn't go to church. Lisa wanted God's priorities to be her priorities. That's always the best way.

Wouldn't it be wonderful, if or when you get engaged, everyone in your life, including your pastor and your Christian grandmother, is excited for you because you've chosen a man who loves Jesus, and who loves his bride, the church?

8
The New Convert

Spiritual immaturity; spiritual disparity; emotional immaturity; instability—all of these things describe the dangers a woman faces as she dates a brand-new convert.
- Kris Swiatocho & Cliff Young

Brothers and sisters, I could not address you as people who live by the Spirit but as people who are still worldly—mere infants in Christ. I gave you milk, not solid food, for you were not yet ready for it. (1 Corinthians 3:1–2 NIV)

In the same way maturity in life is important, a maturity in Christ, both personally and relationally, is extremely significant—especially when it comes to being involved in a serious relationship. . . . Just because two people carry the label "Christian" doesn't mean they are equally yoked.
- Swiatocho & Young[1]

An egg cracks. The shell is broken apart in bits and pieces around a hole that has formed. With some considerable effort, a brand-new chick pops his head out, and squeezes his lanky body out of the eggshell. A baby bird emerges. Mostly naked with a few sparse feathers, eyes initially closed, this chick meets the world for the first time. What will it take for him to survive? How quickly will he grow up? Initially, this baby bird is completely dependent on the momma bird for survival. Not surprisingly, he stays close for warmth and food, and she guides, protects, and feeds her newborn.

Christians go through something similar. For every believer, there is a day when they are spiritually born-again, and immediately become dependent on spiritual parents—or even more importantly, a whole community of believers in a local church—for survival. Baby Christians don't do well on their own, but need the guidance, instruction, protection, and care of shepherds and mature Christians.

In this chapter, we want to consider the problems with marrying someone who just became a Christian. Should a single Christian woman date someone who was just recently saved? Are there any potential problems with this? What do you think?

Darren and Lydia

Darren met Tom through his job. Both worked at a local newspaper, Tom as a reporter, and Darren in sales. At first they had a cordial relationship, but over time, as they discovered common interests, they started spending more time together. After a few months, conversations between the two of them included Tom's favorite topic—Christianity. "Do you believe in God?" "What is truth?" "If you died, what would happen to you?" These were important questions and honest conversations. Darren was challenged to re-examine his worldview, and started reading the Bible with Tom. A few months passed and Darren's desire to know Christ grew. On October 15 of that same year, Darren awoke one morning with a deep desire to ask for forgiveness and give his life to Christ, and so he did.

That Sunday, he went to church with Tom, who introduced him to the pastor and several other church members. After a few weeks of attending, Darren joined the church and jumped into a small group. That's where Lydia entered the picture.

Lydia had a radical conversion to Christianity after her friends witnessed to her in college. Her atheism crumbled under the weight of the gospel. Lydia marveled at the reality of a loving God who sent his Son to die on the cross for *her* sins. Her faith took off, and she quickly grew in her relationship with the Lord. The day that Darren walked into the small group, she noticed him right away—she found him quite attractive. Initially they talked casually, and often found themselves, after a small group finished, standing outside of the church talking for longer periods of time.

A few months and many small group meetings later, Lydia found herself smitten with Darren. For his part, he would flirt with her, text her, and call her, but never asked her out on a formal date. Lydia loved the attention, and she knew she had a choice to make—allow herself to be vulnerable and to play along, or to ask him what was going on between the two of them. She chose the former because she didn't want to risk losing a good thing. A few weeks later, Darren did ask her out to lunch, and they started spending even more time together.

Fast-forward a few more weeks. From all appearances, Darren and Lydia were dating, but Lydia didn't know for sure because Darren had not communicated his intentions. Their relationship took on a more physical nature—holding hands, hugging, kissing—and she didn't mind. She really enjoyed the more intimate side of the relationship. She enjoyed the affection Darren showed toward her. She enjoyed the physical touch and even started to long for it.

Sue, a close friend of Lydia's, pressed her because Darren and Lydia were growing emotionally and physically entangled with one another, and yet Darren had just become a Christian a few months prior. Lydia understood the concern, but honestly she didn't care. Her dream—a responsible, hard-working Christian man, who took a strong interest in her—was finally materializing after years of struggling in dating relationships. Darren went to church and small group consistently. He professed faith in Christ and read his Bible. She loved spending time with him, and they seemed to get along splendidly. So why should she care that he was a new convert?

Things to Consider When Dating a New Convert

There are a few cautions in dating a new believer. The first is that he'll be *spiritually immature*. To be immature is to be more childish in your thinking and actions; to not show godly wisdom, discernment, and thoughtfulness in how you live your life. You'd expect a new convert to show immaturity in a lot of areas of life, simply because he hasn't had time to grow in his faith. This reality was true of Darren, who was often impatient, didn't show discretion in the kind of movies he watched, made inappropriate jokes at times, and still needed to clean up his language. These things were changing and would continue to change, but they would take time.

The apostle Paul writes to the Christians in Corinth:

> Brothers and sisters, I could not address you as people who live by the Spirit but as people who are still worldly—mere infants in Christ. I gave you milk, not solid food, for you were not yet ready for it. Indeed, you are still not ready. You are still worldly. For since there is jealousy and quarreling among you, are you not worldly? Are you not acting like mere humans? For when one

says, "I follow Paul," and another, "I follow Apollos," are you not mere human beings? (1 Corinthians 3:1–4 NIV)

Paul does not treat the Corinthian Christians as mature believers ("spiritual people"), but instead, he calls them "people who are still worldly." They are weak or baby Christians, "mere infants in Christ," whose need for spiritual "milk" shows the immaturity of their faith. Baby Christians drink milk because they are not ready for the solid food of mature believers. Paul is frustrated by this because the Corinthians should have matured in their faith long ago. Instead, they ". . . are *still* not ready" for solid food. Their problem? They are still worldly, that is, living more like the world than as believers in Christ. Their jealously, quarreling, and bickering about leaders ("I follow Paul," "I follow Apollos") shows the immaturity of their faith.

This contrast sets up a criterion for a boyfriend—is he immature or mature in his faith? A brand-new convert is, by definition, immature. He's still a babe in Christ. If you are dating a new convert, is he discerning and wise in his approach to life? Is he more worldly than godly in his thinking and living? Immature believers have worldly desires, thoughts, and behaviors. They value more of what the world values, and less of what God values.

An immature believer understands the most basic elements of the Christian faith, but doesn't have a depth of biblical knowledge. He doesn't have the discernment to navigate his own Christian life yet, let alone to lead someone else. *The most important thing a new convert can do is focus on growing in Christ.*

Tom warned Darren that in the early months after his conversion a girlfriend could be a significant distraction because of the time and energy it takes to keep a dating relationship going. He wanted Darren to not get sidetracked from Christ, his first love (2 Corinthians 11:1–5). Darren's first priority needed to be to "grow up into salvation" (1 Peter 2:2).

Lydia, as a mature believer, has a responsibility to recognize this—that Darren's spiritual growth should take priority in his life. Breaking up (if she would consider it) would be for his good, not just for hers. She needs to be careful that she is not prioritizing her dreams of dating and marriage over his spiritual growth.

The other dilemma for Lydia as she dates Darren is the *spiritual disparity* between the two. Lydia is much more mature in her faith. Yet, in regards to gender roles, the Bible calls Darren to lead in the relationship

(Genesis 2:15–25; Ephesians 5:21–33). *Immature* believers make *immature* decisions. In the future, if Darren makes an immature decision, Lydia shouldn't be surprised. Picture a twenty-five-year-old man, with the spiritual immaturity of a one-year-old. That's what Lydia has to deal with—a one-year-old Christian in a twenty-five-year-old's body. Lydia should expect mistakes and immature decisions along the way. Staying with Darren means Lydia would have to be patient. He would need time to grow up in his faith.

Lydia's other caution is Darren's *emotional immaturity*. As someone grows in spiritual maturity, the character traits that make him mature and wise (1 Corinthians 13:4–6; Galatians 5:22–23; 1 Timothy 3:1–7) will also make him more attuned to the emotional needs of others. Darren would sometimes be insensitive to Lydia's feelings, putting his job first ahead of his relationship with her.

Lydia also needed to be aware of the *instability* that comes with tying yourself to someone who is not mature. The apostle Paul warned believers that they should strive to grow in Christ so that "we may no longer be children, tossed to and fro by the waves and carried about by every wind of doctrine, by human cunning, by craftiness in deceitful schemes" (Ephesians 4:14). Picture yourself sitting in a rowboat in tumultuous waters. As the boat rocks up and down, back and forth, up and down, back and forth, the waves crash overboard, and you get drenched with water. Children don't have the strength, maturity, and wisdom to withstand a treacherous storm. This is not unlike your relationship with a brand-new convert. He'll be tempted to be more worldly than distinctly Christian in his thinking. He's not stable in his doctrine, but is more liable to be "carried about by every wind of doctrine." He's not yet consistent in his thinking, decisions, and planning, so every wind of doctrine that blows in, or human schemes or deceitful thinking has the potential to throw him off. Do you want to get into this boat?

Spiritual immaturity, spiritual disparity, emotional immaturity, and instability—all of these are problems that women can face if they date a brand-new convert.

Why Would Lydia Settle?

That's the key question, isn't it? Why? What's going through her mind? Picture an Olympic-trained high jumper in a track and field meet. If you've ever seen one of these guys perform, you might marvel at how high they can jump. The world record currently stands at eight and a half feet, set in 1993.

Darren has passed the low bar in dating—you must be a believer in order to get married. A woman's mindset can therefore go something like this—"So long as he is saved, we'll be fine because we've met the biblical criteria. Now no one can say that I married a non-Christian. And now I get my dream—a man, a family with children, a house with a white-picket fence, and everything else that comes with marriage."

Lydia would be wise to wait to date Darren. She should recognize that Darren's growth as a new believer will be less hindered by the distraction of a dating relationship. Her dreams of marriage may blind her to Darren's spiritual and emotional needs, but she ought not to let that dream rule her heart.

How about you? When you are in a dating relationship, does the guy's spiritual well-being matter to you first and foremost? Are you more eager for him to meet up with someone to disciple him than to go on a dinner date with you? Are you more enthusiastic for him to read his Bible than to call you? Are you more eager for him to serve in the church's hospitality or children's ministry than sit in church with you? Are you more eager for him to know the Lord than to know you? Do you want him to focus most of his time and energy on Christ or on you?

How William Waited

William was a brand-new convert in the same church as Darren and Lydia. A few months after he was born again (John 3), he developed a strong interest in Lauren. Lauren was a mature believer. She had a clear love for Christ, a fruitful ministry in their church, and quite significant for William, she was also beautiful both inside and outside.

As a brand-new convert, William approached Tom, who was also discipling him, and asked him for his thoughts on whether he should ask Lauren out on a date. Tom told him to wait. "Go to church, build good Christian relationships with other men, read your Bible, and wait." Tom went on to say, "The most basic posture of a Christian is waiting." Just as we all wait in anticipation of Christ's return, so also Tom wanted William to wait on a dating relationship so that William could focus on growing in Christ.

"How long?" William asked.

"At least six months. Probably more."

William waited. He went to church; built good Christian relationships with other men; read his Bible; and waited.

Sixth months to the day since he and Tom had that first conversation, William came back and asked Tom, "What about now?"

I won't tell you exactly what Tom said, but I will tell you that several years later, William and Lauren are now married.

When a Baby Bird Learns to Fly

It takes a while for a baby bird to be ready to venture out on his own. About two weeks after he has hatched, he leaves the safety and comfort of the nest and ventures out, testing his newfound skills. In those early days, he often stays near his parent, not wanting to venture too far, but eventually, he flaps his wings, and takes flight.

In the same way, there is a time when every newborn Christian needs to keep first things first—to focus on his relationship with Christ and to not be distracted by a dating relationship. As hard as it is for him (and for her) to wait, this sets a much better foundation for the many years ahead, since Christ is to be central to everything in his life, including marriage.

Keeping first things first, and second things second is not always easy. To say that dating and marriage is secondary to Christ is no light thing. Since Christ is our Lord, he should be Lord over every inch of our lives. We are called to worship and follow him from the very first days in our journey with him. Like the newborn chick who ventures out of the nest, so also as a man grows in Christ, there comes a day when getting married is a good thing. The safety and comfort of a man's relationship with Christ has allowed him to grow in responsibility and possibly take on a wife.

Don't be impatient and marry the new convert. Be patient and trust that God knows best. If you are already dating a new convert, take a break, and give him the chance to make Christ his first love.

9

The Unbeliever

Any Christian foolish enough to date an unbeliever is foolish enough to marry one! –Melody Green[1]

Do not be unequally yoked with unbelievers. For what partnership has righteousness with lawlessness? Or what fellowship has light with darkness? What accord has Christ with Belial? Or what portion does a believer share with an unbeliever? (2 Corinthians 6:14–15)

If the believer in the marriage holds on to a robust Christian life and practice, the non-believing partner will have to be marginalized. If he or she can't understand the point of Bible study and prayer, or mission trips, or hospitality, then he or she can't or won't participate alongside the believing spouse in those activities. The deep unity and oneness of a marriage cannot flourish when one partner cannot fully participate in the other person's most important commitments. – Kathy Keller[2]

Imagine a little girl, staring at a cookie jar, knowing she shouldn't eat any cookies. She knows what she wants—a mouth-watering chocolate chip cookie. She also knows what the rules are—her mother told her no snacks before dinner—but her desire is to play by her own rules.

Now imagine a grown woman, who goes to church and loves Jesus, but she also wants to be married. She meets a man who doesn't love Jesus, but he likes her. Her friends, her pastor, even the Bible tell her to not get romantically involved with this man, but she does it anyway. She knows the "right" thing to do, but she also wrestles with certain desires (the hope of getting married and having children) and fears (she's scared of being alone for the rest of her life). Which matters more to her—Jesus, or getting married to this man? Which does she desire more?

In this chapter, we consider why a single Christian woman should not date or marry a man who is not a Christian. If you are single, you probably have a friend who has done this, or considered it. Maybe you are considering this yourself.

An unbeliever explicitly rejects Christ. Maybe he is an atheist, agnostic, or nominal in some other faith, but regardless of what he does or does not believe, what is clear is that he has not put his faith in Christ. Is dating or marrying a non-Christian okay with God? Is there a wise way to be with someone who doesn't care about Christ like you do? Or is it foolish to even consider this?

Peter and Sarah

Peter met Sarah at a community barbecue. They had never talked before, but they were standing next to each other in line and struck up a conversation. They ended up talking the whole afternoon, and Peter asked if they could go out for dinner sometime. Sarah quickly responded "yes!" Peter was good-looking, easy to talk to, and best of all, he made her laugh. She really liked to laugh and enjoy life. So why wouldn't she say "yes"?

Things went really well on the first date, so after lots of texting, emailing, phone calls, and a few more dates together, they officially became boyfriend and girlfriend. By now, all of their friends knew. Peter was kind, thoughtful, responsible, good-looking, and a lot of fun to be with. Sarah couldn't believe her luck in meeting Peter. Surely God was looking down and smiling on her.

Sarah grew up in a devoted Christian home, with a mother and father who loved the Lord. She heard the gospel all of her life, and had asked Jesus into her heart at a very young age. She was active in church, youth group, and Christian summer camps. She read her Bible often; and when she got to college, she was just as involved in church and had a solid group of Christian friends.

After a few weeks of dating Peter, she invited him to church, and he happily accepted. He went. He sang along with her; and dutifully listened to the sermon. She introduced Peter to several folks after church, and then they headed out to lunch.

That's where her dilemma began. When she asked Peter what he thought of church, he told her "religion was not his thing." If she wanted to be religious, it was fine with him, but he wasn't interested in a relationship with God. They got along so well together, he didn't see why her religion should get in the way. He liked her a lot, and was hoping to one day marry her.

What do you think? If Sarah were your friend, what would you say? Should she keep dating him? What are her parents going to say? Maybe the Lord might convert Peter? If so, should she stick it out and see if he changes? If Peter doesn't change, is this going to be a problem for Sarah if she gets married to him? There are a lot of hard questions for Sarah to sort through as she considers what to do.

Can an Ox and a Rabbit Plow a Field Together?

Let's start with the biblical standard for marriage. The Bible says Christians should not marry non-Christians. They should *only* marry another Christian.

In 1 Corinthians 7:39 (NIV), the apostle Paul addresses Christian single women, and tells them that if they get married, they should marry men who "belong to the Lord."[3] Marrying a non-Christian is not okay with God. Paul makes clear that if you marry, you *must* marry a Christian.

When Christians quote verses from the Bible about not marrying a non-Christian, most of the time they go to 2 Corinthians 6. Take a moment to read 2 Corinthians 6:14–7:1. The main point of this section is that Paul is making a plea to Christians in the Corinthian church to live holy lives (6:14, 17; 7:1). False teachers (whom Paul calls "unbelievers") had infiltrated the Corinthian church and were influencing the Christians with ungodly, worldly thinking. The key verses for our conversation are verses 14 to 15:

> Do not be unequally yoked with unbelievers. For what partnership has righteousness with lawlessness? Or what fellowship has light with darkness? What accord has Christ with Belial? Or what portion does a believer share with an unbeliever? (2 Corinthians 6:14–15)

Paul lived in an agricultural society, so he picked an illustration that would be common in his day—plowing a field with two animals. Melody Green explains the imagery:

Picture if you will, two oxen tied together at the neck by a wooden crosspiece so they can pull a plow. They are two animals of the same species who have been joined together to do a specific job. They have been carefully trained to respond to the same commands, and once they are united, they are considered to be a team. A wise farmer picks two animals of similar size, strength, and temperament because he knows they will work the best together.[4]

To be "yoked" is to form a joint partnership that is so significant it shapes our identity.[5] When Paul tells a Christian to not be *unequally* yoked, he is warning Christians against forming a harmful partnership— an alliance with someone who is your spiritual opposite. He is saying, "You must not get into a double harness with unbelievers." As one author puts it: "Those who bear Christ's yoke (Matthew 11:30) cannot share it with others who deny Christ. Those who harness themselves together with unbelievers will soon find themselves plowing Satan's fields."[6]

While the main point of 2 Corinthians 6:14–7:1 is a Christian's pursuit of holiness and not being influenced by false teachers who teach worldliness, a secondary implication can be made about alliances with unbelievers. A fundamental part of marriage is being a good team together—being "yoked" together.[7] A strong, intimate partnership with an unbeliever is going to be hard, especially because what a Christian values (righteousness, living in the light, following Christ) differs from what ultimately matters to a non-Christian. The most intimate of partnerships is marriage—where two individuals become one (Genesis 2:24). Paul is warning Christians to not tie themselves to unbelievers because a marital alliance will be much more difficult when you disagree on the most fundamental matters of life—God, sin, faith, and Christ.[8]

Picture two strong oxen, harnessed together, plodding along, as they pull a plow across a field. Now replace one of those powerful oxen with a rabbit. How do you think an ox and rabbit would do together in plowing the field? It would be a disaster. I'm pretty sure the farmer wouldn't even bother trying.

In verses 14–15, Paul follows up the basic admonition to not be unequally yoked with four questions ("For what partnership has righteousness with lawlessness? Or what fellowship has light with darkness? What accord has Christ with Belial? Or what portion does a believer share with an unbeliever?"), all of which warn against making unholy alliances.

He's trying to drive home his point—don't form an alliance with someone whose beliefs differ from your faith. It will be a spiritual disaster.

Partnerships Matter

Paul warns against forming an alliance with unbelievers because he knows how significant partnerships can change you. Committing yourself in marriage to an unbeliever will unduly influence you.

In his day, Solomon was considered the wisest king in the whole world (1 Kings 10:23). He wrote hundreds of thoughtful proverbs and many other significant writings (Song of Solomon, Ecclesiastes). He answered questions from great foreign dignitaries who came far and wide to test him (1 Kings 10:1–13). He administered justice in various disagreements among the Israelites (1 Kings 3:16–28). And yet Solomon's downfall was his disobedience to God's command not to marry unbelieving wives. The Lord warned Solomon that his unbelieving wives would persuade him to worship false gods (1 Kings 11:2).

With all his wisdom, surely Solomon would listen to God's warning! Sadly, he didn't. The next part of the verse says that Solomon "clung" to his wives "in love" (v. 2). When emotions and love take over, logic, clear thinking, and obedience to God's Word often go out the window. Solomon eventually turned from the Lord because of his unbelieving wives. "For when Solomon was old, his wives turned away his heart after other gods, and his heart was not wholly true to the LORD his God, as was the heart of David his father" (v. 4).

If Solomon, the wisest king in the world, could be influenced like this, what makes you think you can resist the influence of an unbelieving spouse? Don't risk your faith in God by marrying someone who doesn't love the Lord.

What about Evange-Dating?

Regardless of what you think about an ox and a rabbit plowing the field together, or Solomon's marriage to foreign women, the reality is that some Christian women date non-Christians. They *evange-date*, which Zach Schlegel defines as "dating a non-Christian in hopes that they will become a Christian while dating."[9] That way, they don't break any of Paul's guidelines. As long as he is a Christian by the time they get to the altar, everything will be okay.

Why do women evange-date? This can be tempting for a number of reasons: they might spend a lot of time with non-Christians at work, school, or in their neighborhood. They might be getting more attention from non-Christians than Christians. Maybe they became a Christian while they were dating and it became hard to break up.[10]

Regardless of your reasons, you shouldn't date a non-Christian. Let me give you six reasons that are worthy of consideration.

First, *the ends do not justify the means.* The most common argument folks make to justify dating non-Christians is to reference situations where the guy ended up becoming a Christian while dating, and their marriage seemingly worked out. Hear me on this—not every story works out. For every situation about a guy who was converted, there are two stories where the guy didn't become a Christian. There is no guarantee that your boyfriend will become a Christian. Salvation belongs to the Lord (Jonah 2:9), not you. Ultimately, you can't make him a Christian. Only God can change someone's heart.

Second, *evange-dating confuses dating with evangelism.* "It is a good desire to see someone trust in Christ, but mixing a dating relationship with evangelism can be confusing and clouds the decision of the person considering the claims of Christianity."[11] How does the guy distinguish between romantic feelings for you and his affections for Christ, when he is exploring both things at the same time? There is a real danger that these two things will be blurred in his own mind and heart. You can't see into his heart and know for sure if he chooses Christ *for himself*, and not just so he can *be with you.* There is a real danger that he will think he is genuinely choosing Christianity, when in fact, in the deepest recesses of his heart, what he wants is to be with you. And to be with you, he knows he has to become a Christian. Sadly, in many of these cases, months or years after they are married, the guy's pursuit of Christianity wanes, and eventually he no longer reads his Bible, goes to church, or cares about following Jesus.

Third, *a casual approach to dating leaves you vulnerable to marrying a non-Christian.* Every marriage starts out with a simple date. If you have a casual attitude about dating like Sarah did with Peter, then you'll be open to going out with non-Christians. God has established a standard—a Christian should only marry a Christian—so believers should never "play the field" and explore all of their options in dating. If we trust God, then we trust that his restrictions in dating are not a burden, but are good for us. As Melody Green warns: "Any Christian foolish enough to date an unbeliever is foolish enough to marry one!"[12] If Christianity really matters to you, then why would you not pick a life-partner who is like-minded with you?

Fourth, there is a danger *you will start compromising your faith in order to get the rewards that come with commitment*—marriage, a man who commits, no longer being lonely, children, a home, sex/intimacy, and a future together. God becomes secondary to all of these things. The longer you are with a non-Christian guy, the more likely you are to get emotionally attached. And the more emotionally attached you are, the more likely you are to compromise on faith issues in order to keep the relationship and eventually get married.

Atheists or agnostics who do not like Christianity will dissuade you from faith and maybe even morally compromise you. A non-Christian guy doesn't care about the Bible, so he doesn't care about the Bible's prohibitions against premarital sex. Some guys will expect intimacy and sex to be a part of the dating relationship, and sadly, you compromise because you know this helps to keep the relationship going.

Fifth, *the point of dating is to find a Christian spouse.* If this is true, then why bother dating a non-Christian? Someone might say, "It's just recreational dating." Anyone you date, however casually, remotely, or infrequently, is a possible candidate for marriage.[13] Another might say, "But he is so nice, kind, responsible, fun to be with, and good-looking" (like Peter in our story above). No matter what good qualities you find in a guy, it doesn't justify going against the Bible. Rationalizing that things will be fine because he will change later on when you are married is probably not realistic. Change doesn't get any easier with marriage. Just the opposite—if he is not open to faith while dating, he will be less likely in marriage.[14] *Ultimately, faith is the most important quality in a husband. If he doesn't trust Christ, then you should ditch him.*

Sixth, *you will have to face the consequences of your disagreement.* When you are ready to bring your children to church with you, and your future spouse says, "no," what are you going to do? Maybe you are dating an agreeable non-Christian, who says he doesn't care, and you can do whatever you want. What if he changes his mind later on? Children suffer when parents can't agree on how to raise them. A parent's example is probably the most important influence in shaping a child's understanding of a loving heavenly Father. Consider Melody Green's warning:

Children usually transfer their feelings and impressions of their earthly father over to their idea of who God is. If their father is a righteous man and exercises godly judgment balanced with love and encouragement, then their image and understanding of God will most likely be good. *(Eph. 6:4; Col. 3:21)* If he is unfair in his judgments, or an agnostic or indifferent to God, then they will have a hard time (even as an adult) seeing God's true nature and character.[15]

If you disagree about foundational beliefs, it will affect not only the children, but other important decisions—how you both spend your time, what commitments you make, what you value. A non-Christian doesn't value the things that God values, and his priorities will show up in how he handles your marriage. He might not want to focus time and energy into the marriage, but focus on other things, like work or hobbies or travel. He might not care about sacrificing his life for you, but rather feels like you need to meet his needs, or else. What if you get pregnant unexpectedly, after you thought you were done having children, and your non-Christian husband wants you to get an abortion? What would you do then? You might argue that these are extreme examples, and your guy is much too kind-hearted to ever do anything like that. But beware—when your faith is at odds with your husband's lack of faith, conflict is inevitable, and you will have to choose whether to follow Jesus or your husband.

Digging Down a Little Deeper

If you were to dig a little deeper into the recesses of Sarah's heart, what you would find is that she knows what the Bible says, she knows what her pastor and her parents think, she knows the passage about not being unequally yoked, she knows Peter is not a Christian, she knows that he may never become a Christian, she knows that choosing a non-Christian husband is turning her back on what God says about marriage, she knows what she is supposed to think, but . . .

Her *desire* for marriage, for a life-partner, and for children trumps her love for God.

Her *fears* about loneliness or childlessness matter more than her worship of Christ.

Her *excitement* over the opportunity to spend her life with Peter matters more than anything she reads in the Bible.

Her heart sings, "This is life!" "Don't give this up!" "Happiness is coming! Peter loves you!" "Look what the future might hold!" She hears the sound of wedding bells. And all this "noise" drowns out the still, quiet, loving voice of Christ.

Take a moment and consider—is this you? Can you relate to Sarah's desires, fears, and hopes? Here is your spiritual battle: Do you believe that Christ is sufficient for you, or do you believe that he is insufficient to meet your needs and you must meet those needs yourself?

I promise you that Jesus *is* sufficient, but do you trust him to be so? Because Christ is sufficient, would you be willing to give up a wonderful guy if he doesn't follow Christ? If you are not willing to give up the guy, what does that say about who is first in your life? What does that say about what matters most to you?

Sarah is tempted to settle for Peter because he's got so many attractive qualities—he is kind, thoughtful, responsible, good-looking, and a lot of fun to be with. In her mind, it's not "settling." She considers herself fortunate, because in comparison, she knows lots of girlfriends who married guys who are jerks. Peter is not like any guy she has ever known. His lack of faith is a problem, but not a big enough problem to stop her from moving forward. His good qualities far outweigh the faith problem, or so she thinks.

What's a Wiser Way to Handle a Relationship with a Non-Christian Man?

Consider Rebecca's approach to this same problem.

Christopher met Rebecca at work. They had the opportunity to talk on several occasions, and he really enjoyed getting to know her. He found her attractive, so he asked her out on a date. She quickly declined.

"You're a nice guy, but I can't date you."

"Why not?" he asked.

"Because you are not a Christian."

He was floored. What does Christianity have to do with anything? All he wanted was a date. He kept talking to Rebecca, only to find out that she grew up in a Christian family and was committed to only marrying a Christian. Christopher was agnostic, and wasn't planning on pretending to be something he was not in order to get a date. Rebecca offered to bring him to church, and surprisingly, he took her up on the offer. The sermon that Sunday was on the judgment of God through the Old Testament book of Nahum. Christopher was completely undone. He had never heard anything like this before in his life. He came back for more in the weeks that followed, and clearly was eager to keep learning. Christopher began to seek God.

At this point, Rebecca had a decision to make—should she keep talking with Christopher and spend time with him as his friend? Inevitably, because they worked together, they would see one another and have some conversations. So, to make the question even more precise, should Rebecca be Christopher's *primary* conversation partner about spiritual matters? In order to not confuse the affections that Christopher had for Rebecca with his growing interest in Christ, Rebecca asked a godly man from her church (Bill) to meet up with Christopher, to be his friend, and to help him sort through his spiritual questions. At this point, Rebecca could back off and let Christopher's pursuit of Christianity be built around conversations with an older godly man, Bible study, and church.

She didn't want Christopher's pursuit of faith to be dependent on her. That would increase the likelihood of confusing dating and evangelism. If she was the primary conversation partner, she would be taking on the role of a spiritual mentor. She wanted to be careful, so that his spiritual growth could survive apart from her. If she took the lead early on in the relationship, there was a danger that his spiritual growth would be more shaped around her than around Christ.

Rebecca waited patiently. She wasn't willing to enter a dating relationship until he was a Christian. She knew the risks of evange-dating, and she was courageous enough to say, "no." That meant, first and foremost, that Christopher needed to be saved—he needed to repent of his sins (Mark 1:15; Acts 3:19) and trust in Christ as his Lord and Savior (John 3:16; Romans 3:21–26). Only after he was converted was she even willing to consider dating.

But that still leaves us with the question, "How does she know he is not faking it or just doing it for her?" Rebecca's confidence could come from a few things—after his conversion, the shape of Christopher's whole life was transformed. He didn't just say, "I believe in Christ," but it was noticeable that he *loved* Christ by the way he pursued faith. On his own, Christopher built relationships with other Christian men. He eagerly read his Bible. He joined a weekly small group, and he was in church regularly. Best of all, none of this was because Rebecca suggested or asked him to do it. Christopher pursued these things because this was what his mentor Bill and the pastor said were important for him to grow in Christ.

Rebecca handled this situation with both wisdom and faith. It was clear from her actions that she cared more about Christopher's faith than she cared about getting married. She knew that even after Christopher became a Christian that it was advisable to wait and see if this was a conversion of convenience—the guy did it because he knew he had to?[16] Or if it was a true work of God—where the Lord had transformed Christopher's heart and turned his life upside down?

Suppose Christopher was converted, got baptized, and went to church with Rebecca, but nothing else really changed in his life—he didn't read his Bible or build relationships with other Christian men; he didn't make it to church regularly, etc. While his words professed faith, his life didn't show it, and as the Scriptures tell us, genuine faith should manifest itself in action (James 2:14–26).

While they were dating, Rebecca came to me and asked, "How can I know for sure that Christopher's conversion is genuine?" Ultimately, she couldn't know for sure since she wasn't God, and she couldn't look into the recesses of Christopher's heart. But she could grow in some confidence by asking Christopher about his motives for following Christ. Rebecca asked him, "If I were to die today, would your faith in Christ survive? Are you doing this for me, or for God?" Christopher was clear in his response, "If you were to get hit by a bus and die today, I'm not giving this up. I love Christ more than I like you!"

Does the Bible Really Matter to You?

If you are a Christian, that means you acknowledge that God has authority to shape and define your life. Practically speaking, how does he do that? Through his fully-inspired Word, the Bible. Do you live as if the Bible really does have authority over your life? If it does, then you will do everything you can to bring your life into alignment with what it says. It is not just words on a page. It is not like any other book you own. This book is the book of books—because it is God's Word addressed to you.

Just consider the ways that Sarah could reject God's authority in her life.

She could outright ignore the Bible's teaching on relationships and marriage and go at it her own way. Maybe she is very busy with Christian things—she goes to church, maintains Christian friendships, and even reads her Bible daily. Nevertheless, when it comes to relationships, she turns to her culture for guidance rather than to God's Word.

If she didn't feel required to live under the teachings of the rest of the Bible, she could conveniently throw overboard the apostle Paul's writings in 1 Corinthians 7:39 and 2 Corinthians 6. Sarah was on a very slippery slope, where a seemingly innocent first date led to emotional attachment, and then to changing her views on the Bible in order to maintain the relationship. If the apostle's words no longer mattered to Sarah, she was free to date and even marry a non-Christian, in spite of its clear prohibition in Scripture.

If Sarah chooses to ignore the Bible's teachings and to turn to the culture to get guidance for her relationships, she is functionally denying the Bible's authority in her life. She is living as if God is *not* sovereign. *To deny God's Word is to deny his authority.* It's to deny him the rightful rule he has in our life as both our Creator and Redeemer. When someone denies God's sovereignty, often what results is living according to their own rules. And that's not a good way for any of us to live. Why should you deny God his just place as King and sovereign over your life?

10
The Angry Man

A man who cannot control his temper before you're married, will most certainly be a man who cannot control his temper after you're married. In most cases, it will worsen. . . –Debbie McDaniel[1]

Make no friendship with a man given to anger, nor go with a wrathful man, lest you learn from his ways and entangle yourself in a snare. (Proverbs 22:24–25)

If the guy you are dating has a tendency to fly off the handle, either at you or others, don't be tempted to rationalize his behavior. He has a problem, and if you marry him you will have to navigate his minefield every day to avoid triggering another outburst. – J. Lee Grady[2]

You and your boyfriend are talking. Your conversation turns a little tense, and you push him to open up to you. He doesn't. He's clearly frustrated with you. As you keep pushing, he explodes—a volcanic eruption with hot and angry words spewing everywhere. You are surprised because you've never seen this side of him before. You don't know what to do. The thought of marrying an angry man fills you with fear.

What should you do? What advice would your friends give you if they knew your boyfriend struggled with anger? Does it matter? Does the Bible have anything to say about it? What if he is a good guy, who occasionally struggles with anger? Would that change anything?

In this chapter, we consider the dangers of tying yourself to an angry man and the implications his anger has for your marriage and children.

Fred and Maxine

Maxine had grown up in church and so had Fred. She became a Christian in college and spent much of her life in church. Every time the doors of the church opened, she had shown up. At first in children's ministry, then youth group. There were church banquets, singing in the children's choir, serving food at the homeless shelter, and going to a Christian school. For Fred it was almost the exact same story. He grew up in the same church, so they were very familiar with each other. They had never had an interest in each other, though they shared lots of mutual friends.

But something changed. They had finished college and were now working responsible jobs—Maxine selling insurance; Fred as a chemist at a local pharmaceutical company. A couple of friends were talking after the church service, and she joined in the conversation. Fred walked up and for the first time, he caught her attention. They talked with one another and laughed at each other's jokes. Some kind of chemistry had begun. After that encounter, Maxine had a hard time getting him out of her mind.

The next time they ran into each other at church, they talked longer, and it was clear they were both interested in each other. Fred liked Maxine. Her no-nonsense personality, her long, curly red hair, and her beautiful eyes were all very attractive to him. She was easy to talk to, fun to be with, and often cracked a sarcastic joke. He liked that about her. Unlike some other women he'd spent time with at the church, Maxine had a lot of life to her. So they dated for about a year.

In that time, Maxine found a lot to like about Fred too. He was responsible, charming, and thoughtful. He planned out all of their dates with the precision and pinpoint accuracy of a research chemist (which he was!). Most importantly for her, not only was he fun to be with, but he led her in spiritual conversations. Every Sunday after church, he would start a discussion about the sermon.

But Fred also struggled with anger. Not all of the time, but often enough that it became evident to her. On their sixth date, she cracked a joke, not knowing it would be offensive to him, and she could see anger boil up inside of him. For a moment, he looked like he was going to explode. He got up, walked away, and came back a few minutes later very composed. She wasn't sure what to do, so she played it safe—she left it alone.

About four months into dating, they got into an argument, and Fred just unleashed on her. He gave himself over to his anger and lit into her, saying things he would later regret. "Are you really that dumb?" "How dare you question me?" "I can't believe you would say that. That's stupid!"

She was hurt, confused, and scared. It took them days to work through it. From that point on, Fred's anger continued to rear its ugly head in the relationship. The long periods of peace were littered with sudden explosions of anger. Maxine didn't know what to do because she liked Fred, but she also was scared to marry an angry man.

How Does the Bible Explain Fred's Anger?

While there does exist a righteous anger (a "right" anger that is not tainted with sin), that only occurs in two ways. First, there is such thing as *divine anger*.[3] God never sins, so when he is angry, he is angry for the right reasons (Mark 11:15; Romans 12:19). He's angry at our sin and our rebellion against him (Psalm 2:4–5). He is also angry at injustices in this world, and dislikes the plight of the disregarded lame, blind, and poor (Luke 14:21). Second, there is *human righteous anger*. Human beings can also get angry for appropriate reasons. For example, if someone abuses a child, it should stir up a righteous indignation toward the abuser. A Christian is right to be angry at the abuser because of his wrong. But in a fallen world, human anger is often tainted by sin. Righteous human anger is much more rare than *sinful human anger*. The apostle Paul warns us—"in your anger do not sin" (Ephesians 4:26; Colossians 3:8). Human anger is tainted by selfishness, self-righteousness, and pride. We get angry because we're offended at someone's comment, we feel someone treated us unjustly, or we didn't get what we want out of a situation.

The Bible speaks to the issue of anger. What does it say?

Slow to Anger

An angry person gets enraged quickly. There is a rush of adrenaline, his emotions flood his system, his heart rate increases, his blood pressure rises, and his muscles tighten. He thinks, *I didn't deserve this!* or *That's unfair!* He raises his voice, turns red, slams a door, or even walks away. Anger rules his heart and his life.

The Bible's warning is to not let anger rule you, but rather to be "slow to anger." Here is a sampling of verses from the book of Proverbs:

- "Whoever is *slow to anger* has great understanding, but he who has a hasty temper exalts folly" (14:29).
- "A hot-tempered man stirs up strife, but he who is *slow to anger* quiets contention" (15:18).

- "Whoever is *slow to anger* is better than the mighty, and he who rules his spirit than he who takes a city" (16:32).
- "Good sense makes one *slow to anger*, and it is his glory to overlook an offense" (19:11).

Even in this small selection of verses, we see how God's Word exalts the great benefits of being slow to anger. A man who is slow to anger has great understanding (14:29), quiets contention (15:18), shows better self-control of his spirit and emotions than a mighty warrior (16:32), and has good sense (19:11). Don't you want these things to describe your future husband? They won't if you marry someone who consistently explodes in anger.

Even better, God himself, when he lists his own attributes to Moses, describes himself as "slow to anger."

> The Lord passed before him and proclaimed, "The Lord, the Lord, a God merciful and gracious, *slow to anger*, and abounding in steadfast love and faithfulness . . ." (Exodus 34:6)

Now if God is slow to anger, wouldn't you want your husband to be like God (Ephesians 4:24; 5:1)?

The Destructive Impact of Fred's Anger

Notice the destruction being quick to anger brings, both to others and to oneself.

> Scoffers set a city aflame, but the wise turn back anger. (Proverbs 29:8)

Imagine an angry man in the middle of a city riot.[4] In an already bad situation, scoffers and mockers only make things worse. They enrage the crowd, and in turn, put a city in perilous danger ("set a city aflame"). The wise control their emotions. In a riot, they control their anger, and are level-headed for the sake of preserving the city and containing a difficult situation. If Fred were in the middle of a riot, would Maxine be embarrassed at his behavior? Would he further enrage the crowd?

> "A man of wrath stirs up strife, and one given to anger causes much transgression." (Proverbs 29:22)

"For pressing milk produces curds, pressing the nose produces blood, and pressing anger produces strife." (Proverbs 30:33)

Just as naturally as churned milk produces curds, or a pinched nose produces blood, so also an angry person characteristically evokes strife and conflict. If Maxine wants a relationship typified by conflict, she should marry Fred. Peace will be elusive to her.

Know this, my beloved brothers: let every person be quick to hear, slow to speak, slow to anger; for the anger of man does not produce the righteousness of God. (James 1:19–20)

James's exhortation is to be quick to hear God's Word (1:22), slow to speak, and slow to anger. This is the exact opposite of the proverbial fool, who is rash in his words (Proverbs 29:2) and unwilling to listen patiently (Proverbs 18:2). James warns that anger does not produce a moral life that is pleasing to God.[5] It actually prohibits a godly life. As he traces out in the rest of his letter, anger produces a loose tongue (3:1–12) and even murder (4:1–3). When a man is angry, he is not listening to God, nor obeying him. He is more concerned with the perceived injustice done to him.

The Dangers of Relating to an Angry Man

If Maxine chooses to stay in the relationship with an angry Fred, the book of Proverbs gives her a few other warnings.

A man of great wrath will pay the penalty, for if you deliver him, you will only have to do it again. (Proverbs 19:19)

The man characterized by anger will have to deal with the consequences ("penalty") of his anger—people withdraw from him out of self-protection; others feel resentful; still others lash back. The caution offered is not to rescue him from these consequences, lest you find yourself having to deliver him again and again. Why is that? A man ruled by anger faces a lifetime of destructive consequences because he repeatedly finds himself in fresh trouble. A spouse lives with the recurrent mess created by her husband's consistent anger. Do you want that to be you?

Consider another warning for Maxine to ditch Fred:

Make no friendship with a man given to anger, nor go with a wrathful man, lest you learn from his ways and entangle yourself in a snare. (Proverbs 22:24–25)

Unlike someone who occasionally struggles with anger, this warning is about someone who is controlled by ("given to") anger. The principle is simple—if you tie yourself to an angry man, you will learn his angry habits and get entangled in his rage.

Assessment of an Angry Person

What's the difference between a man who is controlled by anger, and the rest of us, who occasionally encounter moments of anger, but it doesn't rule our lives? If you're dating someone, and you're concerned about his anger, look at the questions below to see if you can distinguish between the former (a man ruled by anger) and the latter (occasional anger that is not characteristic of a person).

1. Does anger characterize the man you are with? Does it define him? Does it rule his life? Is this typical of him?
2. How often does he get angry? Is it consistent, frequent, or common for his anger to be injected into your relationship? Or is his anger inconsistent, infrequent, or rare?
3. Is conflict common in your relationship? How does he handle a fight—does he calmly work through it with you, or is it typical for him to get angry at you? How often is he escalating a small disagreement into all-out-war? Remember the warning of Proverbs 15:18: "A hot-tempered man stirs up strife, but he who is slow to anger quiets contention."
4. Does he struggle to understand you? Is his lack of understanding because he gets angry quickly, and so does not take the time to listen to you? Consider Proverbs 14:29: "Whoever is slow to anger has great understanding, but he who has a hasty temper exalts folly."
5. When he gets angry, how often does he give full vent to his anger? Does he blow up at you? Consider the warning from Proverbs 29:11 (NIV): "Fools give full vent to their rage, but the wise bring calm in the end." Or is his anger of a different flavor—when he is mad, is it an ice-cold anger, where he withdraws or ignores in order to punish?

6. Is he often critical or harsh toward you? Is he disrespectful and reckless with his words? Think about Proverbs 15:1: "A soft answer turns away wrath but a harsh word stirs up anger."

7. Is he prideful and self-righteous? Is it typical of him to blame you for what went wrong? Do you find that in conflict he is rarely willing to admit his wrong and he presses you to confess your sin? Apply Jesus's words to the situation, "Why do you see the speck that is in your brother's eye, but do not notice the log that is in your own eye? Or how can you say to your brother, 'Let me take the speck out of your eye,' when there is the log in your own eye? You hypocrite, first take the log out of your own eye, and then you will see clearly to take the speck out of your brother's eye" (Matthew 7:3–5).

8. Does he blame his anger on circumstances or make excuses for his anger? ("It was a hard day." "I'm under a lot of stress.") Does he blame his family? ("I act this way because that's what my parents did . . . ") Is he pointing the finger elsewhere for his anger, and unwilling to own his sin?

9. Does he get angry at sin (as biblically defined) or at his perceived injustices?[6]

10. In the midst of raging emotions, is he preoccupied with himself, or is he focused on what concerns God? Is he grieved that the name of the Lord is dishonored, or is he personally offended and hurt?

11. If he struggles with anger, does he know it, humbly admit it, and show an eagerness to fight it? Does he have the tools to manage the anger when it boils up in a fight? Does he know how to handle his anger in a godly way? Does he express his anger in a Christian way—rather than exploding and raising his voice, he calmly and graciously tells you what is wrong?

12. If you are not sure how to answer any of these questions, have you asked the folks who know him best? What would they say about him?

Some of you might be reading this and think, *Oh, no, he's an angry man.* If it's clear to you that he is ruled by anger, then you must decide if you are willing to forbear with his anger for years to come if you marry him. That's a very difficult life ahead if you choose it.

For many of you, as you work through these questions, the answer may be less clear. If this is your situation, question number 12 is most important. You should prioritize seeking out those who know him well. Do they see a pattern of anger that characterizes his life?

We always want to leave room for repentance. What if you are in a situation where a man knows he struggles with anger, but he *actively* fights it with redemptive means of grace (godly tools), like consistent time in the Word and prayer, sitting under the preaching of God's Word, accountability in a local church with close Christian friends and church leadership, a willingness to humbly admit his wrongs and ask for forgiveness, and an eager desire to put the anger away? Then your choice is whether you are going to marry a man who struggles with anger but seems to have the godly tools to fight it. Tying yourself to an angry person is dangerous (Proverbs 22:24–25), but the good character qualities consistently demonstrated by this man (Galatians 5:22–23) and his demonstrated pattern of humbly fighting his anger might make marriage a viable option. *Repentance is necessary for a good marriage.* Let this man show that he can contain his anger, and make it an increasingly rare event in your relationship.

Whoever you marry will be a sinner. Choose a man who takes God's side against his sin, though not perfectly, but earnestly.

The Volcano Grows Cold Over Time

What would it look like if Fred came to terms with his anger? It would start with Fred taking an honest look at his walk with Jesus, and seeing where his relationship fell short. To fight anger, he'd need to be renewed in the gospel daily. He'd need his relationship with Jesus to be sweet, not intellectual. He'd need his affections for Christ to grow. Walking with Christ needs to be more than head knowledge. The best prescription for fighting anger is not anger-management techniques, but a growing love for Christ.

He also needs to be humble enough to recognize his need for help. Anger destroys relationships and homes. Humility for Fred would mean taking his anger issues to the Lord, and then seeking out other brothers in Christ to walk alongside of him. It would be foolish to think the problem would go away immediately. Accountability would be crucial in the battle against anger. Fred can show Maxine he's committed to getting help by initiating conversations with godly men rather than having them track him down after things go poorly in their relationship.

He also needs to read the Bible so that he can understand God's perspective on anger and how to fight it. Then, when anger does come, if the Spirit brings conviction of sin, he will quickly apologize for his wrong and reconcile with Maxine.

Along with that, Fred would no longer tolerate a pattern of anger. If it continued, he'd plead with God to give him the strength to obliterate the pattern. If a pattern of anger developed, there would be sin in his life, and it would need to be dealt with in order to prevent him from ruining his marriage and family. He'd be quick to confess. And he'd ask for help. He wouldn't tolerate a pattern of getting angry at his wife or kids, or raising his voice. There would be no screaming. He'd learn to cool down before he speaks harshly. He'd learn to deal with the self-righteousness in his own heart before he attacks his wife. He'd be more concerned with God's perspective than his own perceived injustices. He'd learn to hold his tongue because he knows the venom that spews out when he's red-hot.

It is possible for Fred to fight his sinful anger and become more Christlike. If Maxine were dating Fred, and asked me what to do, I'd tell her to not marry him until she (and the rest of her confidantes like her close friends, older women who are discipling her, and her pastor) see clear evidence that he'll learn to control his anger *prior to* engagement or marriage. That means she'll need to be patient and wait. Otherwise, she'll one day find herself trapped in a living nightmare.

Why Did Maxine Settle?

The dangers of marrying an angry man should be no surprise to you, but women still do it all the time. Why? What makes a woman settle, even after she's been exposed to the man's anger?

It's easy for Maxine to remind herself of the good things and suppress the bad parts of the relationship. If Maxine's hope is in marriage, she'll remind herself that Fred shows kindness to her, he is organized and responsible, and most importantly, he leads in spiritual conversations, including talking about the sermon every Sunday after church. "He's a good guy," she'll tell herself. Alongside of this, her rationalizations for his anger creep in—"It doesn't happen all the time," or "After all, he's a Christian, right?" As if the label of "Christian" somehow justifies his anger.

It's also easy for Maxine to tune out the warnings of friends. Friends noticed Fred's anger. Some of her closest friends heard her describe a few of their nasty fights and they expressed their concern. Even though it sometimes took days to work through, Maxine would come back to her friends with—"We're reconciled, so we're good." Somewhere deep down inside of her, she knew that Fred's anger was a problem, but she wasn't willing to heed the warnings of her friends. She started to share with her friends less, and in turn isolated herself (Proverbs 18:1), because she wasn't willing to give up her desire to get married. She rejected the sound judgment of godly friends who saw the warning signs of an angry man and spoke to her about it.

Why? Because she wanted marriage, a husband, children, her dreams attained, intimacy, sex, and a future together. If God really loved her, he'd give her what she wanted, right? She never explicitly said this or consciously thought this, but she lived as if it were true. She would often think, "Doesn't God want me to be happy?" Sadly, Maxine was not seeing the difficulties that come when you are married to an angry husband.

The Destructive Effect of an Angry Husband in the Home

As you date someone, you will naturally ask the question: "Can I see this man as my husband?" In the case of a boyfriend who struggles with anger, consider for a moment the effect of his anger on your future home.

Anger sets the tone of a home. If a father is ruled by anger, the wife and the children will live in fear of the father's wrath. They orient their lives around not upsetting their father. Your home life will be characterized by fear and intimidation, not love. There will be limited seasons of peace, punctuated by volcanic eruptions. Each explosion will throw the entire household in turmoil.

If you are struggling with your boyfriend's anger, ask yourself: Do I want this for my kids? Do I want him treating my kids in the same way he treats me? You might immediately rationalize this with a thought, *He would never do that to our children*, but don't be fooled. If he is willing to do this to you, what makes you think he won't also let loose on your children? A man who lacks self-control makes a mess in almost every part of his life, not just with you.

Hiding Yourself in Dating

In dating, the norm is to put the best foot forward. Get dressed up. Look nice. Be happy. Don't share anything too deep or too revealing. Get to know the person. That's what you expect early on in dating. Because you are trying to win the person over, to convince them that you are worthy of their time and attention, you are more self-controlled.

The danger in writing a chapter like this is that some guys will do a good job of hiding their dark side. You might see glimmers of his worst sins in dating, especially if you are together for a while, but essentially he saves the best stuff for you, and does a good job of covering up everything else.

In marriage, you are in a permanent relationship, so each of your true colors come out. For some women, sadly, the worst parts of a man's life only emerge as they begin the honeymoon. I had a woman recently tell me, "The first time he cursed at me or told me to shut-up was after we got married." Until then, he was nothing but sweet to her.

What can you do about this? Is there a way to avoid this problem? Other people who know you and love you and your boyfriend can be a great help. Let other Christians into your relationship—a pastor, a discipler, close friends, your parents, and really anyone in your church whom you trust to be wise and godly. Let them get to know you and him. Let them see the relationship and see how the two of you relate to one another. Invite others to be involved. Ask them to help you. A church community is meant to be a cooperative of Christians who recognize they are sinners in desperate need of God's grace, and who see *both* God's Word and God's people as a means by which God provides help to us. If you don't have others involved, who can you turn to today to get advice, counsel, and support? Is there a wise, godly person that comes to mind? If you don't know them well, could this be an excuse for you to get to know them better and to ask them for their help? Are you concerned that you might be a burden to them? If you are, then take some time to read the "one another" texts of Scripture (John 13:34–35; Romans 12:10; 13:18; 15:7, 14; Ephesians 4:2, 32; 1 Thessalonians 5:11) to see the role of Christians helping each other out in the Christian life.

The End of this Matter on Anger

The apostle Paul writes in Romans 12:

If possible, so far as it depends on you, live peaceably with all. Beloved, never avenge yourselves, but leave it to the wrath of God, for it is written, "Vengeance is mine, I will repay, says the Lord." (vv. 18–19)

Sinful anger is retaliation for a perceived wrong, a denial of something you wanted, or a blaming of another person. The one who struggles with sinful anger avoids the spotlight on his sin, personalizes the hurt, and reframes it as an injustice done to him. In this light, it's easy to self-justify or to rationalize anger, and to say the other person deserves what they got.

Sinful anger is never *just* before a *holy* God. Vengeance belongs to God and God alone (v. 19). Our responsibility is to "so far as it depends on [us], live peaceably with all" (v. 18). The choice of peace might be to marry a man who struggles with anger if he is employing godly tools to restrain it, and has demonstrated a consistent pattern of control *before* you get engaged. Or it might be to break up with your angry boyfriend because you know how poisonous anger can be to a relationship and to a future home.

Ditch the angry man. Don't give him the time of day. And you'll find that you have a much better chance at living a peaceful life.

11

The Lone Ranger

*Christian men need to see discipling and accountability
as essential to their spiritual life.*

*To love at all is to be vulnerable. Love anything and your heart
will be wrung and possibly broken. If you want to make sure of
keeping it intact you must give it to no one, not even an animal.
Wrap it carefully round with hobbies and little luxuries; avoid
all entanglements. Lock it up safe in the casket or coffin of your
selfishness. But in that casket, safe, dark, motionless, airless, it
will change. It will not be broken; it will become unbreakable,
impenetrable, irredeemable. To love is to be vulnerable.*
– C. S. Lewis[1]

Whoever isolates himself seeks his own desire; he breaks out
against all sound judgment. (Proverbs 18:1)

In the 1950s, the television show *The Lone Ranger* enthralled the hearts of
Americans. Actor Clayton Moore played the Lone Ranger, a masked man
who fought injustice in the Old West with his Native American sidekick,
Tonto. Every episode was filled with action, intrigue, and some kind of
dilemma that needed solving, which led the show to become ABC's first
true hit and the highest rated television program in the early '50s. Oper-
ating almost singlehandedly, the Lone Ranger solved dilemmas and then
rode off into the sunset while someone would ask, "Who was that masked
man?" And the answer would be, "He's the Lone Ranger!"

Many young men have grown up thinking that being a strong man
means being a "lone ranger," and they apply this outlook to their Christian

faith. Consequently, churches today are filled with lone rangers—single men who attempt to singlehandedly take on their Christian faith, without realizing the grave danger they are in. These men have a deficient understanding of Christian relationships and undervalue building their life around a local church. Such immature men make poor husbands.

The purpose of this chapter is to encourage you to stay away from a lone ranger. As I've argued in the first few chapters, the signs of immaturity are there. You just need to keep your eyes open and not overlook these faults in your pursuit of marriage.

Jonathan and Savannah

Jonathan first met Savannah at a church cookout. Struck by her beauty, he talked with her for nearly two hours, and was smitten from the very beginning. She was a Southern belle, immaculately dressed, even for a summer picnic. Having grown up in Georgia, her accent was as thick as molasses, and her conversation was littered with "y'all," "Bless your heart!" and a thousand other Southern phrases.

Jonathan called the very next day and asked her out. Savannah quickly said yes, and a day later, they found themselves on a dinner date, sitting across from each other, and enjoying another long conversation. They told a lot of stories, laughed out loud dozens of times, and found they shared a lot in common. The night went so well they saw each other every day in the coming week. Two weeks later they were officially dating, and Savannah gleefully shared the news with her girlfriends.

Being an outgoing person, Savannah knew everybody at church. She often stayed after services and talked with as many people as she could. Jonathan didn't know that many folks, so he usually stood around while Savannah had conversations. At first he was patient, but with time, it irritated him. Before Jonathan had met Savannah, he made small talk for a few minutes and then quickly headed out the door.

About a month into dating, Jonathan and Savannah were talking over dinner, and the conversation hit the hard topic of relationships in the church.

Savannah started off, "Why don't you like it when I stay after church to talk with people?"

Jonathan shrugged his shoulders. "I don't mind it sometimes. It's just frustrating when I have a lot to get done after church and need to wait for you."

"Why don't you talk with people? You don't know that many people in church, do you?"

Feeling a little pressure from her questions, he replied defensively, "I know some."

Savannah frowned at Jonathan's vague answer. "Who do you know?"

"Well . . . I've sometimes had conversations with Tony."

Savannah's eyes narrowed. "That's it? There are four hundred people in our church."

"I also talk with the pastor on my way out the door."

There was silence for a few moments. Rather than dropping it Savannah pressed further, "Don't you want to get to know more people?"

Irritated with the line of questioning, Jonathan started to get frustrated. "Well . . . uh . . . maybe . . . what's with the interrogation?"

Savannah put down her utensils, and looked directly into his eyes. "I'm concerned. You don't seem to be all that connected with folks at church. And it doesn't seem like you care."

"Ouch. That hurts. Who made you the expert on relationships?"

"Sorry. But I'm just trying to be honest. Are you part of a small group?"

"No."

"Why not?"

Jonathan thought about her question. "Because I don't have the time."

Aggravated, Savannah leaned forward, starting to motion with her hands as she spoke. "You've got plenty of time. There are several nights a week when you are at home emailing, reading, checking Facebook, or exercising. Surely you can spare one of those nights to meet up with some other guys?"

"I could, but I don't want to. Look . . . I read my Bible, I go to church, and I'm learning a lot about following Christ through the sermons. I'm doing just fine, so can we just drop this whole thing?"

A little miffed at Jonathan, Savannah let out a sigh and moved on to another topic.

A High Value for Christian Relationships and Church Life

What should you (as a single woman) expect of a Christian man in regards to his relationships? Typically, people will say things like, "Watch closely to see how he treats his mother." That's good practical advice, because if he cares well for his mother, it shows in how he honors her

(Ephesians 5:1), taking time out of his schedule to love, support, and serve her (1 Timothy 5:8; 1 John 3:16–18).

But is that all God expects of a single man? Let me suggest four things that every single woman should look for in single men when evaluating their relationships.

First, *Christian men need to see relationships as vital to the Christian life.* As image-bearers, God has made men to be in relationships, first with him, but also with others (Genesis 1:26–28; Mark 12:29–31). Regardless of whether he is an introvert or an extrovert, a Christian man grows in faith and love in the context of loving, redemptive relationships. Faith in God is never any good in isolation from other Christians. Whether he likes it or not, those relationships are *necessary* for his spiritual growth. The apostle John makes it clear that you can't claim to love God and not also love your brothers and sisters in Christ (1 John 4:19–21). Many times, it is the friction of real relationships that spurs us on to greater faith in God (Hebrews 10:24–25).

Second, *Christian men need to see discipling and accountability as essential to their spiritual life.* Take a quick look at the "one another" verses in Scripture, and you find that Christians have an obligation to be invested in each other's lives (John 13:34–35; Romans 12:10; 13:18; 15:7,14; Ephesians 4:2,32; 1 Thessalonians 5:11). Discipling is the ministry of doing spiritual good for another Christian so that he might grow in greater faith in Christ. It includes studying Scripture, and praying with each other, but it doesn't stop there. A discipler will share his life with his friend, learning together what it means to follow Christ. Older Christians open up their lives to younger believers. They give younger men an opportunity to learn through what is "taught," but also in what is "caught" by sorting through life together (2 Thessalonians 3:7; Hebrews 13:7). In the context of Christian discipling (or other relationships with Christian men), a single Christian man grows in transparency with other men, allowing them to hold him accountable for sin, faith, dating, work, church life, and many other aspects of his life (Proverbs 28:13–14; James 5:16). Accountability involves Christian men asking each other hard questions, confessing sin to each other, and consistently following up to encourage integrity and faithfulness.

Third, *single Christian men should also see accountability to authority as important.* The author of Hebrews makes this very clear,

> Obey your leaders and submit to them, for they are keeping watch over your souls, as those who will have to give an account.

Let them do this with joy and not with groaning, for that would be of no advantage to you. (Hebrews 13:17)

Despite our anti-authoritarian culture, a Christian man understands that loving authority is a good thing when he puts himself under it. He makes himself accountable to his leaders and shows humility by following their instruction. As a woman, the last thing you want is to be in relationship with a man whom church leaders consider a burden (literally, they groan about him) because he is continually bucking authority and trying to get his own way.

Fourth, *Christian single men should also value involvement in a local church.* The author of Hebrews also declares:

And let us consider how to stir up one another to love and good works, not neglecting to meet together, as is the habit of some, but encouraging one another, and all the more as you see the Day drawing near. (Hebrews 10:23–25)

The author of Hebrews expresses concern because some Hebrew Christians were neglecting to gather with the rest of the church. An essential ingredient in growing in faith in Christ is regularly gathering together as a church.

Christians can't live in isolation from one another. That's spiritually dangerous. The web of relationships in your local church is meant for your good. Those relationships help you to persevere in faith in Christ, especially when things get difficult.

You will see if a man values church if he is willing to build his life around a local church. Why would he do so? Because he understands the close connection between church involvement and his spiritual growth.

Why Is Jonathan the Wrong Guy?

What did we learn about Jonathan? Like many who have bought into American individualism, Jonathan's faith centers around his personal relationship with Jesus Christ. Before Savannah entered his life, Jonathan lived an isolated life. He was not involved in church or solid Christian relationships.

Jonathan didn't see the need for other Christians in his life. He has spent much of his Christian life surviving on his own. Sure, he went to

95

church every week. But he wasn't invested in relationships. He didn't see why he needed other Christians if he was doing fine on his own.

Jonathan didn't see the need for deeper involvement with the church. He approached the whole venture of church as *an individual*—as if his survival in this life was dependent exclusively on him. Fueling his individualism was his pride, i.e., an "I-can-do-this-on-my-own" attitude. He also approached church as *a consumer*. He went to church to get things, not to give or serve or love. He went to church to listen to the sermon and to learn more about God and faith through the services, but not to help anyone else out. What Jonathan didn't realize is that *he needed the church*—that relationships in a local congregation were vital for his faith. Faith grows in the context of redemptive relationships. It is part of God's wonderful plan for Christians to sort through the trials of life by journeying hand-in-hand with other believers. Individualistic, consumeristic Christianity is an anathema. There should be no such thing.

In a funny kind of way, *the church also needed him*. I once had a friend say to me that if a young man can spout off Bible verses or doctrine, that doesn't at all convince him that this man is a Christian. But if that same young man is willing to pick up an older widow to drive her to church, or to clean up after a wedding reception, or to serve in childcare, he shows that his faith means something. He doesn't just know God in his head, but his love for God shows itself in his actions (James 2:14–26). It will show up in how he engages in relationships and loves other Christians. How does the widow get a ride, or the reception hall get cleaned, or two-year-olds get cared for in the nursery? When Christians—including young, single men like Jonathan—learn to grow in Christlike love as a part of the body of Christ in a local church (2 Corinthians 12:12–31; Ephesians 4:12–13). The church needs Jonathan just as much as Jonathan needs the church.

Jonathan is a loner. He doesn't see the need for others, and because of that, he doesn't do the hard work of developing deep, meaningful Christian relationships. When he gets together with friends, they talk about work, sports, and weather, but no one asks any deeper questions. Real Christian love is not *comfortable*, but is willing to be engaged with one another and take risks. Genuine Christian love is not *convenient*, but is willing to be inconvenienced for the sake of Christ.

Jonathan doesn't demonstrate a love that cares for God's people and sacrificially serves the church. Jonathan doesn't see the need for discipling or accountability. Jonathan isn't engaged with the leaders of his church—they don't know who he is because he never sticks around long enough for them to get to know him.

What if you married Jonathan? What do you think might happen? It doesn't take the gift of prophecy to figure out what is likely to be your future. If Jonathan's attitude toward relationships doesn't change, Jonathan and you would live separate lives in regards to church. He would do his own thing while you would be very involved. He might attend church regularly, but would not have any meaningful relationships with the pastors or any men in the church. If he doesn't value these things now, there is nothing (apart from the work of the Spirit in him) that is going to necessarily change any of this in the future. If this is who Jonathan is *right now*, this is what you should expect *later on* in marriage.

In dating Jonathan, Savannah discovered that Jonathan doesn't value Christian relationships. Although they might be wonderful together—they have common interests; they learn a lot about faith from one another; they laugh and enjoy being together—if Jonathan stays isolated from other Christian relationships, especially those in their church, Savannah has set herself up for trouble. She is choosing to follow a man who doesn't value something that is a clear priority in Scripture. And that is always a bad idea.

In earlier chapters, we talked about the importance of not making decisions about dating and marriage on your own, but finding help within the context of Christian community. That means having other people, especially married couples, your parents, church leadership, or anyone who is older and wiser, helping you sort through your dating relationships. How is Savannah to know if Jonathan has good character, will make a good husband or father, understands how to lead a wife, or if he is ready to take on the responsibility of supporting a wife and children? Her ability to figure this out on her own is limited, but she can grow in her certainty of these things when an older and wiser couple, her parents, or church leaders affirm that Jonathan is ready for marriage and is a good choice for a spouse.

In Jonathan's case, this is not possible. He is a guy under no authority, and he rather likes it that way. He does not have any identifiable discipling relationships, either with someone who is discipling him or someone whom he is mentoring. He doesn't have any guys around him who can attest to his godly character. If Savannah decides to marry him, she is doing so based on her own limited wisdom and insight, not based on the wisdom of others who have been involved in his life. That puts her in a very precarious position to make the second most important decision in her life!

A Humble and Teachable Jonathan

You are likely to meet many men, especially guys in their twenties, who are not going to get this. They might have friends, but not deep friendships. They might go to church, but are limited in their involvement and don't work to build their lives around the church. You can't expect a twenty-year-old single man to have the same kind of maturity as a fifty-year-old pastor. We want to give this young guy a chance to grow up.

The ideal is for Jonathan to be plugged into Christian relationships, have ample accountability, and be deeply invested in his church. But short of that, we want to give Jonathan a chance to grow and mature in Christ. What would it look like if Jonathan was humble and teachable?

Let's replay the conversation between Jonathan and Savannah, and see how things might be different if Jonathan was humble and teachable.

Remember, Savannah started off with the question, "Why don't you like it when I stay after church to talk with people?"

Jonathan shrugged his shoulders. "I don't mind it sometimes. It's just frustrating when I have a lot to get done after church and need to wait for you."

"Why don't you talk with people? You don't know that many people in church, do you?"

Feeling a little pressure from her questions, he replied defensively, "I know some."

Savannah frowned at Jonathan's vague answer. "Who do you know?"

"Well . . . I've sometimes had conversations with Tony."

Savannah's eyes narrowed. "That's it? There are four hundred people in our church."

"I also talk with the pastor on my way out the door."

There was silence for a few moments. Rather than dropping it Savannah pressed further, "Don't you want to get to know more people?"

Jonathan thought for a moment. "Well . . . uh . . . maybe . . . Until I met you, no one had ever talked to me about the importance of Christian relationships. I am starting to realize why I need to get more involved with other believers. Maybe you can help me get more connected with some of the men in the church?"

Wow. What a difference. Jonathan is not resistant; he wants to get connected to others, because he has a humble and teachable spirit. With time, he might come to understand the high value of Christian relationships and involvement in a local church. If Savannah encountered this kind of attitude, I'd want to encourage her to patiently help Jonathan connect with other men in the church. Over time, his life will show whether his words were genuine. If he grew in his relationships with Christian men, and started to build his life around the church, Jonathan would make himself a much better prospect as a Christian husband.

Don't Settle for the Lone Ranger

At the beginning of every episode, the Lone Ranger rode in on a magnificent white stallion named Silver, and then rode off into the sunset crying out, "Hi-yo, Silver! Away!" Faced with action and plenty of drama, *The Lone Ranger* was a show viewers loved to tune in to every week.

Go ahead and watch *The Lone Ranger* on TV, but don't date or marry him. He has an immature view of Christian relationships, which, if overlooked, will be costly for you in the future. Find a Christian man who loves God's people and loves being a part of a local church, and you will find yourself in a much better position for marriage.

12
The Commitment-Phobic Man

A commitment-phobic man's "love" is cheap, easy, and immature at best. Ask anything more of him, and he won't give it to you. Anything that comes at great personal cost is too much for him.

Many claim to have unfailing love, but a faithful man who can find? (Proverbs 20:6 NIV)

The Lord God models faithfulness, fidelity, and commitment, the same qualities that a man is called to if he is to be with a woman. This is real love. It's a mature love. It is not cheap and easy; it is costly.

Everyone builds their life on promises. No matter who you are, you get this. From the small ones, like "I'll be home tonight at seven," to the really big ones, like "I want to marry you," real life revolves around the giving, receiving, and fulfilling of promises.

Promises provide greater certainty for our future because they give us something we can rely on. Hannah Arendt reflects, "Promises are the uniquely human way of ordering the future, making it predictable and reliable to the extent that this is humanly possible."[1]

Promises also trace out the parameters of our commitments. A committed and faithful man will make a promise and keep it. He will stay committed to the relationship and be willing to make and keep both little and big promises throughout his life. He is able to do this as he relies on God, who has always kept his promises to him!

In this chapter, I want to warn you to stay away from the commitment-phobic man—the guy who is unwilling to make or keep promises.

He'll use you for his lustful pleasures and his relational needs and then discard you if you ask too much of him. He doesn't understand what it means to stay faithful and committed, to keep his promises, and to put you first, all of which are bedrock for a stable, long-term marriage.

John and Donna

Donna works as a physical therapist. She's reliable, kind, and taller than most of her friends, which as you'd expect, means she tried basketball in high school. She didn't last long on the team because she wasn't competitive enough to survive.

At a young age, she trusted in Christ, and even though things have been up and down in her spiritual life, on the whole, she has desired a relationship with Jesus and been an active part of her church community. Through the years, although Donna had many guy friends, she never dated or had a romantic relationship.

Donna met John at a party. She caught his attention almost immediately after she walked through the door. John liked tall women. He flirted with Donna through most of the night. As you'd expect for someone who never dated, she loved the attention. They exchanged cell phone numbers, and even before she got home, he called her.

Over the next few months, John and Donna spent a lot of time together. Sometime towards the end of the first year, a close friend expressed a concern, "Are you guys ever going to get married?" Donna's answer: "I don't know."

Why doesn't Donna know? John never communicated his intentions for the relationship. Initially, he expressed interest, not by defining the relationship, expressing his intentions, or making a commitment, but by pursuing her for a friendship and spending time together. Conversations were at first superficial. Over time, as she grew in her affection for him, she opened up to him. With time, their communication became deep, intimate, and personal. Eventually the relationship took on a physical side—he held her hand, hugged her at the end of a date, and eventually kissed her, which drifted into making out. Occasionally it slid into premarital sex, though Donna often told him "no." They spent a lot of time together, had daily conversations, texts, or emails, and even sat together in church.

After a while, she got frustrated because she didn't know where the relationship was going, so she finally asked John, "What are we doing?"

A little put off by her question, John responded, "You are my girl-friend; and I'm your guy. We enjoy being together, right?"

"Yes. But that's not my question. We've been together for a year. Are we going to get married?"

A look of panic flashed across John's face. "Marriage? Why did you have to bring up the M word?"

"You don't want to get married?"

"No. I like you a lot, but we don't need to go that far, do we?"

A moment of silence passed; then Donna asked, "Don't you love me?"

"Of course I do."

"Then why don't you want to marry me? We've been together for a whole year . . ." Her voice trailed off. Tears welled up in her eyes.

"Because I like what we've got right now, so don't ruin a good thing." John tensed up, and looked away.

"Look at me . . ."

"What?" John didn't look at her. He stared the other way.

"Don't do this to me." Donna was scared.

"Do what?"

"I've given my life to you for the past year, and the best you can do is, 'We've got a good thing'?" She reached out to touch him, but John pulled back.

John said, "What's wrong with you?"

"I love being with you," tears streaming down Donna's face, as her mascara ran down her cheeks. "But I want more than just a friendship."

Another pause. She asked again, "Don't you want to get married?"

John turned to her, his gaze hard and unmoving. Without any hesitation, he shot back, "No. I don't. Friendship with benefits is just fine with me. If you want more than that, go find another guy."

Donna couldn't take it anymore. She buried her face in her hands and started bawling.

John got up and walked out.

The Danger of Dating a Commitment-Phobic Man

Put yourself in Donna's shoes. Imagine you just found out that the man you had given your life to, with whom you were vulnerable emotionally and physically, who you expected to be your husband, just didn't care about marriage. Would you regret the time you invested in the relationship, especially since he won't commit to anything more than a friendship?

Too many couples make a classic mistake—spending too much time together without ever defining their intentions in the relationship. A biblically responsible man leads by expressing his intentions to the woman from the outset. Clear communication creates clear expectations, and is a vital ingredient for building a healthy relationship.

Many years ago, after I took Sarah (who is now my wife) out on a few dates, I explained my intentions for the relationship. I desired to date her, with the hope of discerning if the Lord would lead us to marriage. And if at any point either of us knew we no longer wanted the relationship, the kindest thing to do would be to end it quickly.

In John's case, he never committed to anything beyond a friendship. Marriage was not an option. A physically-entangled and deeply vulnerable relationship, without any prospect of progressing beyond friendship, is especially dangerous for a woman. She can find herself in a perpetual friendship that is a road going nowhere.

Love Equals Commitment and Faithfulness

Too many couples use the term "love" without ever carefully defining it. Early on in a dating relationship, when a man enjoys being with a woman, he wants to communicate his affection for her. Too many times, I've heard a guy say to his girlfriend, "I love you," yet, what does he mean when he says "love"?

What Love Should Not Be

Our view of love is often shaped by Hollywood movies. Think about the last romance flick you watched—the stirring music, the beautiful people on the screen, the relational chemistry, physical attraction, and sex. Love according to Hollywood is tantamount to a strong subjective feeling. You enjoy being with this person and you find him or her physically attractive. But it's a feeling *without a commitment*. As long as the feeling lasts, the relationship is great. When the feeling leaves, too often the love boat sinks. Don't believe me? Just take a look at the divorce rate, or ask your pastor how many marriages in your church are struggling to hold things together.

John's understanding of love is skewed and selfish. He wants the relationship and all the benefits of a close, intimate, physically-entangled friendship, but without any commitment. As author and love-expert Jonathan Leeman has argued, "Commitment phobia takes commitment out of love and love becomes what's advantageous to me."[2]

Consumerism, individualism, and selfishness are little hobgoblins that attack love and reduce it to its immature forms. Our consumeristic tendencies stare at the face of love and say, "I'm only here to get what I want or need." And even worse, "If I don't get what I want, then I don't care anymore." Our individualism looks in the same direction and boasts, "I can figure this out on my own, I don't need anyone else's help." Our selfishness screams out, "I only care about me." A commitment-phobic man's "love" is cheap, easy, and immature at best. Ask anything more of him, and he won't give it to you. Anything that comes at great personal cost is too much for him. He just won't stick around long enough to see the light of day.

What Love Should Be

One of God's many amazing attributes is *his faithfulness*. From the beginning of biblical history, the Lord God models for us what it means to make and keep promises. In the opening pages of Scripture, after Adam and Eve rebel, God promises that the seed of the woman will one day come to defeat the serpent (Genesis 3:15). He promises never to destroy all of humanity by a flood again (Genesis 9:11); to make childless Abram into a great nation (Genesis 12); and to give his wife Sarai a child (Genesis 15). If the Israelites obey God, they can remain in the promised land (Deuteronomy 28). Even after rejecting God for a human king (1 Samuel 8), God promises to give them an eternal king, one whose kingdom would be established forever (2 Samuel 7). God makes many more promises throughout Scripture (Leviticus 26:11–12; Ezekiel 34:23–24; Jeremiah 31:31–34, etc.), and he shows himself faithful in fulfilling each and every promise. Despite our faithlessness—our tendency to break our promises, and rebel against God, he remains faithful.

One other attribute of God that bears mentioning is his *commitment* and *fidelity* to his own people. If I were God, in my frustration, I would have given up on the Israelites after the first few times they didn't listen. But God is not like me. Instead he persevered with the Israelites. After the Lord freed them from slavery in Egypt, the Israelites showed their ingratitude and forgetfulness when they worshipped a golden calf, complained about their new life, longed for their past, and didn't do what God asked of them. Despite the Israelites' lack of faithfulness to God, he kept his promise to bring them to the Promised Land.

God showed his commitment and faithfulness to his people through the mediators he sent to save them—Moses, Joshua, David, and Solomon, all of whom were a foreshadowing of the greatest of all rescuers, Christ. God's commitment to believers today is shown through his sending his only Son to die on the cross for us. The Israelites, and of course us too, deserve death, eternal punishment, and separation from God for our sin. But in his mercy, he gives us what we don't deserve—a rescuer who paid the price for our sins, giving up his life so we can be reconciled with God (Mark 10:45; 2 Corinthians 5:21). Despite our rebellion against him, God perseveres with us, and remains committed and faithful.

The Lord God models faithfulness, fidelity, and commitment, the same qualities that a man is called to express toward his wife. This is real love. It's a mature love. It is not cheap and easy, but it is costly. So costly that God would give up his one and only Son to die for his children. Every woman should look for a man who desires a mature love, one that comes at great expense to his own life, as he lives out a Christlike self-sacrifice and commitment that turns into a vivid demonstration of the gospel.

What you should expect from a man, at the very least, is that he would be a person of his word. When he makes a promise, he keeps it. He does so because he wants to be a living picture of the gospel, modeling God's faithfulness and commitment to his wife. He is mindful of the warnings of Scripture: "Let your 'yes' be yes and your 'no' be no, so that you may not fall under condemnation" (James 5:12). Pursue a man of integrity who will honor the word he has spoken. "Many claim to have unfailing love, but a faithful man who can find?" (Proverbs 20:6 NIV).

A Stark Contrast

If we pressed the commitment-phobic man for a definition of love, it might come out as: "I really dig this relationship," or "I like you a lot," or "I want to be with you." Like many men, he's looking for a way to communicate his subjective feelings, especially as they grow from a seed to a mid-sized mountain. Sadly though, for a commitment-phobic man, his subjective feelings are all too often swimming in a pool of self-interest. "I'm interested in you so long as this relationship gives me what I want."

A more mature man would define loves as: "I'm confident that we would make a good team so I'm willing to commit my life to you." Mature love is marked by a Christlike commitment to loyalty, self-sacrifice, and fidelity—three words that are not in a commitment-phobic man's vocabulary.

Why Donna Just Couldn't Let Go

Donna settled for a year-long relationship with John—who was consistently vague with his intentions—for two reasons. First, she was relationally and emotionally attached to him. The danger of being vulnerable and emotionally intimate with someone *before* he expresses his commitment is that you will probably end up with nothing. Too many men are unwilling to commit, or prefer to drag out a friendship with benefits, rather than elevating the relationship to something more.

It is always wiser to let commitment precede emotional intimacy, and not the other way around. Why is that? Because love commits. True love understands that faithfulness, commitment, and fidelity are essential ingredients to a long-term stable marriage. Commitment is costly, and a lot of men don't want to make the sacrifice, despite how much they enjoy a woman's company—their relationships never take the next step into a committed, faithful relationship.

Second, the deeper Donna got into the relationship, the more she had invested of herself, and the harder it became to let go. Think of it this way: if you pay one non-refundable dollar to go to a musical concert, and something else more entertaining shows up, you won't mind giving up the dollar. But if you pay three thousand non-refundable dollars to go, and something else comes up, you won't want to skip the concert. You've invested too much to give up on it and do something else instead. So it is with a relationship; the greater the investment, the harder it is to give it up. As Donna might have described it, "I worked so hard, and gave so much of myself, I didn't want to give up. I wanted to do everything I could to make it work."

A Serial Dater

If you looked into John's history, you'd find out that he was a serial dater. Good-looking and charming, he didn't have a hard time getting into a relationship with a woman and taking it as far as he could go. If the relationship ever reached a point where it was too costly, not meeting his needs, or he was getting bored, he'd drop the girl and get out faster than a mouse being chased by a fox. A commitment-phobic man often ends up using his girlfriend and leaving her behind when he is ready to move on.

As pastor and author Jonathan Leeman warns: "What does a fear of commitment do to love? It reconfigures love so that the binding or breaking of commitments becomes less relevant. Loyalty and fidelity are removed from love's ingredients."[3] That's why it makes sense to stay away from a commitment-phobic man. He doesn't understand *real* love. He offers to you a cheap imitation of biblical love, and all too often, he leaves behind a trail of broken relationships.

Do Not Awaken Love

Probably the most famous phrase in Song of Songs is chapter two, verse seven: "I adjure you, O daughters . . . that you not stir up or awaken love until it pleases." When a man and a woman have a mutual affection for each other, it's not unusual for things to move along, and sometimes quickly. But Solomon warns—don't rush love. Don't awaken it before the proper time. The woman speaking in 2:7 is telling her daughters to allow love to proceed at its proper pace.

If a man tells you, "I love you," proceed carefully. If by love, he means to commit his life to you, then what a wonderful future you have before you! However, if by love, he wants a friendship with benefits, then drop him quickly. Once you notice that a man is commitment-phobic, stay away!

13
The Passive Man

God made men and women to work. It's a basic part
of how we are supposed to live on this earth.

The slacker craves, yet has nothing,
but the diligent is fully satisfied. (Proverbs 13:4 CSB)

Families take effort, so when I refuse to exert it,
I am to some extent refusing to be a part of the family. It makes
sense that our wives get upset about that attitude. It makes sense
that something as "small" as not "helping around the house"
could ultimately destroy a marriage. It destroys it because we
aren't participating in it. We have no right to be lazy husbands.
Family is work, marriage is work, life is work, and it's our job
to do it all without complaint. – Matt Walsh[1]

Imagine you are standing in your kitchen, married with two children.
Your husband is on the couch, a room away, reading the newspaper. Your
youngest child starts to have a temper tantrum, and is flailing about on
the floor screaming. Dinner is cooking, and your older child needs help in
the bathroom. You wish your husband would get up and help. He doesn't.
He ignores the whole thing. You're left on your own to deal with it. Again.

You think, *He just doesn't care,* or *Why doesn't he do something?* No one
would want to see herself in this scenario. So how do you get there? Consider how this happened for Hilary.

Tom and Hilary

Hilary is tall, well educated, and works very hard. She grew up in Maine, loves to ski, and keeps herself physically fit. She has a good job teaching at a local college. She is well liked in her community and is good friends with many of her neighbors. She is a proud homeowner and loves gardening in her front yard.

Hilary lived an agnostic life. God existed, but she didn't have any need for him. A neighbor invited her to church a few times, and she politely declined. But her neighbor persisted in asking, and eventually, she said "yes" simply to be nice to her neighbor. The whole experience at church surprised her. The pastor explained a passage from the Bible. Rather than an archaic book with an old message, the sermon was relevant to her personal struggles. Even more surprising was what she noticed about the church members. She expected weak people who used religion as a crutch. Instead she found intelligent, competent folks, who were part of a loving, servant-hearted community. When these people sang hymns, they sang as if they really believed there was a God. When they prayed, they prayed as if they had a personal relationship with the Creator of the universe. When the pastor or other members prayed to God, they talked to him as if he was seated right next to them. After several months of attending church and reading a Bible, Hilary came to faith in Christ. For several years, she faithfully attended and grew in her understanding of the Scriptures and her love for her Savior.

Hilary met Tom at church. He was easy to talk with and they were about the same age. After a few conversations, Tom asked her out on a date, and they met for coffee the following week. Tom was very polite. He did a lot of simple things that impressed her, like opening and closing the door for her. They met for coffee again, and then dinner several times. Eventually they started sitting together in church.

Tom wasn't working. He talked about his hopes of going back to school. He had lost his job a few months back, and had been collecting unemployment to make ends meet. He told Hilary about the things he was hoping to study and the job possibilities that would come if he trained for a different profession.

Although Tom was kind and fun to be around, Hilary noticed that she was often the one to initiate phone calls or texts. She usually set up their dates. Frequently she paid for dinner because she knew Tom was tight on money. None of this really mattered to her. She liked Tom and he clearly liked her. They seemed to be a good fit together. If they got married, maybe she could put him through school and after he got a new job, they could start having children?

Called to Work

In the very beginning, God put Adam in the garden of Eden to work it and keep it (Genesis 2:15). God tasked Adam and Eve with the job of being caretakers, gardeners, and zookeepers—watching over his creation on his behalf, and being fruitful with their hands and their minds.

God made men and women to work. It's a basic part of how we are supposed to live on this earth. Hard work—Adam and Eve's labor in the garden of Eden—came *before* the Fall of mankind in Genesis 3. So, as much as all work is tainted by sin, work in itself is not inherently sinful, but is a good thing.

The biblical authors commend diligence and hard work (Genesis 2:15; 2 Thessalonians 3:11–12; Hebrews 13:16). They encourage us to be productive with our lives, and to learn a trade so we can provide for ourselves and for our family (1 Timothy 5:8). At the same time, the Bible speaks against laziness and idleness (Proverbs 13:4; 18:9; 20:13; 24:30–34). It cautions us not to be sluggards, and warns about the shame, poverty, and ruin that comes if someone is unwilling to work (Proverbs 10:4–5; 10:5, 18; 19:15; 20:4).

When we work, we should work heartily, because we are doing it for the Lord, not for men (Colossians 3:23). That's the main reason why we work—to bring glory to the Lord in all that we do (1 Corinthians 10:31). Some people work because they love what they do. Others work even though they feel ambivalent or dislike their job. Regardless of how you feel about your job, you should work so that you don't have to depend on others, but can provide for yourself and your family (1 Timothy 5:8; Proverbs 31:16).

Did you notice the early warning signs that Tom is the wrong kind of guy for Hilary to marry? Tom wasn't working, so at the time they were dating, he was not capable of adequately providing for a possible family. Even though he had lots of great dreams about his future (education, job possibilities, etc.), he had nothing to show for it yet. Also notice that Hilary is leading the relationship. Why is that a problem? Let me explain.

Tim and Hilary, Part 2

Tim and Hilary did get married. Hilary worked hard to motivate Tim to get the applications for graduate school filled out. He was accustomed to his free time. He didn't want to put in the effort. For months he stayed home and didn't do much. Eventually he did fill out the applications, but only after consistent nagging from Hilary (Proverbs 21:19). After a while, he started graduate school, which they both hoped would lead to a new career.

Then another problem emerged. The date nights and the long conversations stopped. The burdens of daily life—a mortgage, bills to pay, church activities, tending to the house, etc.—made life very full. A few years later, there were two children in the mix, and Hilary and Tim were working hard to keep up as parents.

That's when Hilary noticed. They were spending so much time keeping up with life, that they rarely had time for each other. Their marriage took a backseat to everything else in life. Unless Hilary scheduled a dinner, or initiated a conversation with Tim, he didn't pursue her. After they were done with their work, put the kids to bed, cleaned up the house, and paid the bills, Tim usually did his own thing. If Hilary planned something for the family, he would go along—dinner out, a family vacation, a visit to the grandparents. But he never *proactively initiated* toward her or the family. If there was ever time left in their very full life, he would spend it doing what he wanted to do.

He also never led her or the children spiritually. He didn't offer to pray at meals, nor read the Bible to her or the children. He went to church with the family, but if it were not for Hilary and the kids, she thought that probably he would skip church and stay home.

Tim exhibited passivity relationally and spiritually. That left Hilary feeling very lonely in their marriage.

Passivity Hurts a Marriage and Hinders a Family

If I were to describe to you a continuum of leadership in the home, on one end would be *tyranny*—a strong-willed, controlling husband, who shows very little grace, and rules his home like a micro-managing dictator. On the other side would be *abdication*—a passive husband, who does not lead in his own home, or take much initiative in his relationship with his wife and children. Often the result is that the wife usually steps in and runs the family.

Consider the apostle Paul's words in Ephesians 5.

> Wives, submit to your own husbands, as to the Lord. For the husband is the head of the wife even as Christ is the head of the church, his body, and is himself its Savior. Now as the church submits to Christ, so also wives should submit in everything to their husbands.
> Husbands, love your wives, as Christ loved the church and gave himself up for her, that he might sanctify her, having cleansed her by the washing of water with the word, so that he might present the church to himself in splendor, without spot or wrinkle or any such thing, that she might be holy and without blemish. In the same way husbands should love their wives as their own bodies. He who loves his wife loves himself. (Ephesians 5:22–28)

Christ, the groom, and the church, his bride, are described in the greatest of all marriages. It is the clearest, brightest, and best of love stories, where the groom demonstrates the ultimate act of love by giving up his life for his bride (v. 25). Our human marriages are meant to be a dim reflection of Christ and his relationship with his bride, the church.

Christ sets up an example for husbands to follow. The biblical picture of a husband is one who loves, leads, and initiates for his bride, just like Christ did for the church. In this, the gospel sets a template for our marriages—a husband should be willing to die to himself and give over his life for the spiritual good of his bride (Ephesians 5:25–27).

This is why a husband's laziness and passivity is such a big problem. It sets up a picture of marriage that is the exact opposite of what we see in the gospel. And the wife is left to fill in the gaps where the husband is not leading.

Why Did Hilary Settle?

When Hillary married Tim, she knew what she was stepping into. She was marrying an unemployed man. She did most of the initiating in the relationship. She understood both of these things as she entered into marriage. So why did she settle for Tim?

Reason number one—because Tim talked about further training and a new career. He made predictions and vividly described his hopes about the future. She banked on those things becoming true. She oriented her life around the *possibility* of him working hard, not the *actual reality* of it.

Reason number two—she thought she could change him. Hilary was a natural leader. She was strong, competent, and well-liked by her peers. When she met Tim, and heard he was unemployed, she wasn't concerned. She heard his hopes and dreams about the future and that excited her. She liked hitting goals. She immediately started scheming on how she could help him prepare for a new career. She was convinced she could make him into a better man than he already was.

Reason number three—because Tim was a Christian. He was a Christian so it was biblically permissible for them to get married. Nevertheless, he was an *immature* believer. Hilary found security in the fact that Tim was a Christian and she ignored all of the other warning signs (his lack of a job and lack of initiation in the relationship), because she wanted to get married to him. She was "in love" and that's what mattered most to her.[2] Yet, she suffered the consequences of marrying an immature believer. Because Tim rarely initiated in spiritual matters in the home, that left Hilary to read and pray with the children whenever she could find the time.

Reason number four—because no one had the hard conversation with her and Tim *before* they got married. Ultimately, Hilary and Tim are responsible for their choices, including the choice to get married to each other. But, if I were her pastor or father, I'd tell her not to get married until Tim had an established lifestyle of hard work.

Can you relate to Hilary's situation? Are you with a man who is lazy or passive or both? Imagine saying to yourself, "No, this is not good enough for me." Would you be willing to do that? Or if he is lazy, are you willing to challenge him and see if he will become a hard worker *before* you get engaged or married? If he is passive, are you willing to challenge him to take more initiative in the relationship? Can you relate to Hilary, a competent person who takes the steering wheel and makes things happen? Why shouldn't you? After all, God gave you talent and initiative, right? Of course, there is nothing wrong with moving toward someone in relationship. But there is something wrong with being the one who is always taking responsibility for not only your relationship, but someone else's whole life. That's not taking the initiative, that's enabling a man to ignore God's call to be like Christ in relationship to you. The more you let your guy abdicate, the less opportunity he has to learn to be like Christ in sacrificing his life.

Go Get That Boy

Remember the scenario we started with—a wife in the kitchen, trying to get dinner ready, a child in the throes of a tantrum, and her husband, on the couch, reading the paper and not doing anything to help?

What if this was Hilary and Tim? Let's say that while they were dating, Tim's pastor or Tim's best friend had challenged him to grow in his faith, to get a job, and to learn to lead in the relationship with Hilary. Maybe one of them had the courage to say to Tim, "You can't get married until you get a job and learn to take responsibility for the relationship." What if Tim responded in faith and grew in his work ethic—because "I want to work for the Lord"—and grew in his understanding of what it means to sacrifice his life for Hilary? What if, over the course of time, he learned to take more initiative with her? As he grew in Christ, it would be possible to learn these things, so that Tim could be better prepared to be a godly husband for Hilary.

If Tim loved Jesus more than even Hilary, he'd desire to be more like Christ. He'd grow in taking more responsibility for both his own life and in caring for her. He'd grow in humility and repentance. He'd fill out graduate school applications without her asking. He'd initiate with her and the kids because he wants a spiritually healthy family. He'd take delight in serving his family. He would not do all this out of his own strength—he'd go back to Christ daily and plead with Jesus to sustain him. When he would fight passivity, Christ's power would be shown in Tim (2 Corinthians 12:8–9).

A husband who is relying on Christ for daily help and power to love wouldn't stay on the couch while his wife and children needed him. He would engage his temper-tantrum-prone two-year-old son. He'd do that to serve his wife. He'd do that because the child needed direction. He'd do that because (most fundamentally) he wanted to honor Christ.

If you can see yourself in Hilary and Tim's relationship, take a moment and think about what your future might look like if you marry a passive man. Don't settle. If the guy you are with is passive in life and relationships, care enough to challenge him so you give an opportunity for the Spirit to work in his life. And if he doesn't change, find the guy who is willing to love and serve you, just as Christ gave up his life for his bride.

14

The Unteachable Guy

Whoever trusts in his own mind is a fool, but he who walks
in wisdom will be delivered. (Proverbs 28:26)

*If you think of this world as a place intended simply for our
happiness, you find it quite intolerable: think of it as a place
of training and correction and it's not so bad. – C. S. Lewis*[1]

*A man who does not want counsel and hides from accountability
is a man who is not ready to be open with a wife. He may seem
strong and independent, but he may actually be prideful.*
– Shelley Poston[2]

Imagine yourself as a queen, married to the earth's greatest king, Nebuchadnezzar II. During his reign (606 to 562 BC), he revitalized the city
of Babylon. Famed were the ornate temples, hanging gardens that he
built for you (now one of the seven wonders of the ancient world), and the
outer walls of the city, which were wide enough for chariots driven by four
horses to pass each other.

Let's pick up with his story in Daniel 4 . . .

. . . as the king was walking on the roof of the royal palace of
Babylon, he said, "Is not this the great Babylon I have built as
the royal residence, by my mighty power and for the glory of my
majesty?"

Even as the words were on his lips, a voice came from
heaven, "This is what is decreed for you, King Nebuchadnezzar:
Your royal authority has been taken from you. You will be driven
away from people and will live with the wild animals; you will

eat grass like the ox. Seven times will pass by for you until you acknowledge that the Most High is sovereign over all kingdoms on earth and gives them to anyone he wishes."

Immediately what had been said about Nebuchadnezzar was fulfilled. He was driven away from people and ate grass like the ox. His body was drenched with the dew of heaven until his hair grew like the feathers of an eagle and his nails like the claws of a bird (Daniel 4:29–33 NIV).

Nebuchadnezzar was looking out on the city of Babylon and taking credit and glory for himself—"Is not this the great Babylon *I* have built, by *my* mighty power and for the glory of *my* majesty?" The king boasts about what he has done rather than give the glory to God. That's his sin—a heart ruled by arrogance before the Most High God.

The scary thing is that the king was warned. Just twelve months prior to this account, Daniel said that because of his pride, God would humble Nebuchadnezzar (Daniel 4:24–27). And God kept his promise. With the boasts still fresh on his lips, the king was driven away, went insane, and lived like a wild animal, until he was willing to acknowledge the Lord as truly sovereign over the earth.

Would you marry a guy like this? If you were to get hitched to an arrogant man, even if he is a great king with unfathomable power and riches, you should be prepared for God to humble him, for the Scripture says, "Poverty and disgrace come to him who ignores instruction, but whoever heeds reproof is honored" (Proverbs 13:18).

In this chapter, we will consider why you should not marry an unteachable man—someone who spurns correction because of his pride and arrogance. If you are dating a man like this, be careful. If you marry him, you risk a lifetime of misery. What are the early warning signs? Why would any woman date and marry a prideful, arrogant, unteachable man? How can you make sure this doesn't happen to you?

Stella and Bob

Stella is shy. She's spent much of her life in church. She grew up in a home with an agnostic father and a mother who took her to church every Sunday. In high school she was saved, and walked faithfully with the Lord for many years. She has a decent job as a teacher, owns her home, and loves her church community.

Stella is thirty-eight, and she longs for marriage. She's not had a date over the last few years, and with each passing year, she feels like her dream of marriage is slipping away. Loneliness is painful. Friday nights are hard. She often has no one to spend time with. She's grown to dread attending weddings or bridal showers, because every one of them is a reminder that she lives without any current prospects for marriage. There are plenty of days when she wonders if God has forgotten her. She knows it's not true, but she still wrestles with the thought.

Bob and Stella met at a church potluck. Stella was attracted to Bob instantly, and though there were plenty of other people to talk to, she paid a lot of attention to him, and he got the hint. He asked her out for dinner, and they met up later that week. Dinner went well enough that they met a few more times.

Bob was in his late thirties, and he was divorced. They talked about the circumstances of his divorce, but it didn't bother Stella at all that he had a failed marriage. Bob was good to her, paid a lot of attention to her, and clearly wanted to be with her.

The early signs of problems were there in the relationship. He would always choose what they did on dates. He never asked her what she was interested in doing. She initially attributed this to him being a strong leader, but then she noticed a few other concerns. One time, he was impolite to Todd, an older man at church, and she said something about it. He scoffed at her and criticized Todd. He wasn't open to her correction.

In arguments between Bob and Stella, he was *always* right. During the entire course of their dating relationship, he never relented on a single point. Whenever something went awry, he never seemed to see wrong in himself and was good at playing the victim in an argument. That bothered her, but not enough for her to give up the relationship.

A Spiritually Dangerous Position

Let's consider how the Bible helps Stella to understand Bob's problem. As we look to the book of Proverbs, we meet the characters of the fool and the scoffer, who consistently despise instruction, rebuke, and correction.

> The fear of the Lord is the beginning of knowledge; fools despise wisdom and instruction. (Proverbs 1:7)

> A wise son hears his father's instruction, but a scoffer does not listen to rebuke. (Proverbs 13:1)

The fool often spurns correction and instruction. Because he isolates himself, he focuses on his own desires and ignores what others want. In doing this, the fool despises all sound judgment about whatever issue is at hand.

> Whoever isolates himself seeks his own desire; he breaks out against all sound judgment. A fool takes no pleasure in understanding, but only in expressing his opinion. (Proverbs 18:1–2)

The fool also ignores correction because he is convinced he is right and trusts only in himself. He's not open to advice and instruction from others because he doesn't trust them nor the wisdom they would offer.

> The way of a fool is right in his own eyes, but a wise man listens to advice. (Proverbs 12:15)

As this fool pursues his selfish desires, trusts only in himself, and ignores what others say to him, he shows how much he lacks humility and how much his heart is ruled by arrogance and pride.

Consider the consequences of the fool's pride and arrogance. Probably one of the most chilling verses in the Bible is Proverbs 29:1. The warning to those who consistently ignore reproof is that suddenly, the problem will catch up with them, and they will be "broken beyond healing."

> He who is often reproved, yet stiffens his neck, will suddenly be broken beyond healing. (Proverbs 29:1)

As if that weren't bad enough, God himself will be opposed to you if you are proud.

> Therefore it says, "God opposes the proud, but gives grace to the humble." (James 4:6–7)

Spiritually, there is nothing worse than God being opposed to you. The solution is simple: God calls all of us to humility. Peter (who had his own struggles with arrogance) puts it this way:

> Clothe yourselves, all of you, with humility toward one another, for "God opposes the proud but gives grace to the humble." Humble yourselves, therefore, under the mighty hand of God so

that at the proper time he may exalt you, casting all your anxieties on him, because he cares for you. (1 Peter 5:5–7)

Marriage to an Arrogant Fool

What does marriage to an arrogant man look like?

Stella tells Bob what kind of vacation she wants to take, or what kind of car she prefers, and he picks what he wants. He chooses his desires over hers.

Stella asks Bob to come home in time to regularly have dinner with her and the kids. He chooses to stay late—only sometimes because he has to, but often because he wants to get more work done. She pleads, and at times nags him about this, but he ignores her because he rationalizes, "She doesn't get what it takes for me to be successful at this job." In his pride and selfishness, he is unwilling to heed her pleas to spend more time with the family.

She confronts him when he is overly harsh with the kids. He scoffs at her, especially since he thinks she is not stringent enough with them.

Maybe Bob struggles with anger, or laziness, or pornography, or something else. Whatever his issue, his main problem is not these struggles per se, but *his arrogance toward his struggle*. A man whose heart is ruled by pride and arrogance has a small and weak view of God and a distorted view of his own sin. Because of all of this, his wife's petitions to him for leadership or tenderness or compassion will come up lacking and often unanswered. Because of his lack of repentance and humility, sadly, he will often persist in his struggles.

If your husband is unwilling to make the marriage a partnership, but rather acts like an arrogant dictator of a small country, then the marriage is destined for failure. Either the wife will consistently give in to her tyrant husband's demands in order to keep the peace, which is a miserable position for the wife, or it will end in divorce because it was never really a partnership in the first place.

Why Did Stella Settle?

In the end, Stella married Bob. Why? In her twenties, she felt she had the freedom to date different guys, and to be more picky. In her thirties, Stella went through several years when no one asked her out. With each passing year, her desire to be married no matter what grew, and grew, and grew, to the point that it mattered more than the kind of guy she would marry.

In her early twenties, she would have dropped Bob without any hesitation. But at thirty-nine, she was afraid to let go of the dream of marriage, children, and security, and felt like this was her last chance. She was willing to overlook Bob's faults to attain her greater goal—marriage. After several years of no one asking her out, she was starved for the attention of a man, and didn't want to give up her dream. Fears of permanent loneliness and not ever being a mother, struggles with comparing herself to her peers, and her desire for companionship—all of this made her blind to Bob's faults.

Just consider Stella's own words:

> Do you understand the desperation I feel to just find someone and start this life I've been wanting all these years? Not to mention the life all of my friends and peers *already* have. Since I am in my late thirties, all of my friends have elementary and middle school kids by now, so I'm feeling left behind and can't quite catch up to everyone else.
>
> There is so much pressure to fit into American culture. At a certain point, maybe late twenties or thirties you want to spend your time doing what everyone else is doing—planning family vacation, getting on the PTA, potty training, going to soccer games, planning carpool, shopping at Costco for real and not to just buy one thing. These are all the things my friends complain about but I long for. It's hard to be in conversations or even Bible studies and listen to all of these folks, and feel like you don't fit into their world.
>
> I can't speak for everyone but just the companionship aspect of getting married is very appealing to me, and leads me to date whomever, even though the guy may not be a good fit. The idea of not having to go to events alone or just have someone to plan things with is huge. Even just walking into church by yourself can be hard . . . and that's just church. Not to mention parties, get-togethers, holidays, weddings, etc.

As you hear Stella's struggles, can you relate? Consider whether your desire for marriage looms so large in your life that you are willing to make whatever sacrifice is necessary to get it. How much do your fears define you? Do the fears of loneliness or of not being a mother compel you to lower your standards in picking a future husband? If your boyfriend were not willing to listen to your advice or correction, would that make you concerned about marrying him? (If it doesn't, it should!) Are you desiring at any cost the life some of your friends already have attained—marriage, children, PTA meetings, soccer games, etc.? If you are in your thirties, in what ways are you willing to compromise in order to get married? Are those good compromises?

The King Who Looked to Heaven

Do you know how the account of King Nebuchadnezzar ended? Let's return to Daniel 4, as Nebuchadnezzar describes what happened after he lived like a wild animal:

> At the end of that time, I, Nebuchadnezzar, raised my eyes toward heaven, and my sanity was restored. Then I praised the Most High; I honored and glorified him who lives forever.
> His dominion is an eternal dominion;
> his kingdom endures from generation to generation.
> All the peoples of the earth
> are regarded as nothing.
> He does as he pleases
> with the powers of heaven
> and the peoples of the earth.
> No one can hold back his hand
> or say to him: "What have you done?"
> At the same time that my sanity was restored, my honor and splendor were returned to me for the glory of my kingdom. My advisers and nobles sought me out, and I was restored to my throne and became even greater than before. Now I, Nebuchadnezzar, praise and exalt and glorify the King of heaven, because everything he does is right and all his ways are just. And those who walk in pride he is able to humble. (Daniel 4:34–37)

With nails like the claws of a bird, hair grown like the feathers of an eagle, eating the grass like an ox, Nebuchadnezzar lived like an animal. But as he cast his eyes up to heaven, he showed that he would submit his life to God. He acknowledged that indeed God is sovereign over heaven and earth. With this simple act of looking to heaven, the king repented before God of his foolish pride.

Nebuchadnezzar was the greatest king on the earth, and God would not tolerate a rival, someone who sought to steal his glory. The narrator tells us in verse 37: "And those who walk in pride he [God] is able to humble." The Lord humbled Nebuchadnezzar because he was arrogant. The king's foolishness demonstrated that "pride goes out before destruction, a haughty spirit before a fall" (Proverbs 16:18). But after the Lord humbled Nebuchadnezzar, the king recognized his foolishness, submitted his life to God, and the Lord restored his life. God exalts those who humble themselves: "One's pride will bring him low, but he who is lowly in spirit will obtain honor" (Proverbs 29:23). In the end, because Nebuchadnezzar repented before God, God reinstated his life and his sanity.

Some women mistake pride and arrogance as a strength. They won't date a humble man because they foolishly see humility as a sign of weakness. That's thinking more like the world than like God. In the kingdom of God, humility is a valuable trait. No man is perfect. Because every man you date will make mistakes, it's crucial for him to be teachable and humble (just as it's crucial for you to be teachable and humble!). Pride blinds a man to his own faults, while humility helps him to see his sin, accept correction, and pursue godliness. Who wants to marry an arrogant man who needs to be humbled before God like Nebuchadnezzar?

While you're not likely to encounter a Babylonian king looking for a date, proud, arrogant, unteachable men are much more common. Granted, we all struggle with pride, but some men are ruled by pride and unwilling to listen to correction. If you notice that your boyfriend's heart is ruled by pride, he lacks humility, and won't take instruction from you (or others), don't stay with him, no matter what. It is far better to remain single and wait for a humble man who would make a much better companion, than to be trapped in a bad marriage to an arrogant man.

PART 3:

The Quest for a Godly Man

We've come a long way. Now that you've met ten men whom you shouldn't settle for, you're probably left with a few troublesome questions: *How do I know if this is the wrong guy for me? And if he is the wrong guy, what do I do?* As you face hard truths, you might also face the painful reality that your relationship should end (if you are in one right now). You need help knowing if you should break up and what is the best way to end things.

We have talked a lot about guys who aren't ready for marriage, but what does a godly guy look and act like? While no guy will be perfect, how can you tell when a man has a genuine love for God and you?

What if there is no man like that on the horizon? What if you simply have to wait? Waiting is agonizing on most days, and barely bearable on other days. Why is it so hard to wait? And as Christians, how do we wait well?

Finally, none of this is possible without God's grace. No matter the specific circumstances of our situation, God's grace will get us to the end of the story.

That's the roadmap for what's ahead. This is our final sprint to the finish line, so stick with me.

15

Breaking Up for the Glory of God

As you mull over the ten men from earlier in the book, a few burning questions press in. *Should I stick it out or should I end this relationship? Am I with the wrong guy? What if my head tells me to end it, but my heart refuses to let go?* Wisdom is needed to answer these questions. These are important decisions with lifelong consequences. It's always sad to me when I meet with someone who ignored the concerns of family, close friends, and even what God says in the Bible about the guy she married, only to regret that choice. I'll never forget Donna, who a few days after her wedding day, called her father and said, "I made a *big* mistake."

In this chapter, we'll consider a few criteria to help you decide whether to end it—how to know if you should break up. In examining these criteria, if you decide the relationship should end, think about how to end the relationship for the glory of God.

Why add in "for the glory of God"? Are we just over spiritualizing life? I don't think so. God's glory really does matter (1 Corinthians 10:31). This is not just about you and a guy. You are a child of God, so in everything you do and every choice you make, you are called to honor God. If the best way to follow the Lord is to end this relationship, then do it. But if the best way to follow God is to continue with this man, then do that.

Apart from your own decision to follow Christ, choosing who you will marry is one of the biggest decisions you will ever make. That's why it is so hard to decide. Let's consider some principles that will help you make a wise decision.

How to Know If You Should Break Up

The specifics of your life matter. I don't know you personally, so I can't help you decide if or when to end the relationship. What I can do is imitate Jesus's conversations, where he often answered a question with more questions. The inquiries below are meant to help you evaluate your relationship. If you are not sure how to answer them on your own, get a close friend to help you. Pray together with your wise friend that the Lord will provide clear answers.

Does This Relationship Lead You to Love Jesus More or Less?

All of the other questions matter, but this one matters the most. As a Christian, Christ should be first in your life. Does time with your boyfriend cause you to love Christ? To serve him more? To want to know him more? If the answer is "no," then why would you hold on to the relationship?

If Jesus matters less than this relationship, you may be in danger of worshipping this guy more than Jesus. That might seem overly dramatic, but it is true. What you cherish and value most in your life is what you worship. Does this guy lead you to love Jesus more or to love him more? Does he point you to Christ more than to himself?

Does This Relationship Lead You to Sin More?

Sin is ignoring God's way and going our own way. It's putting ourselves on the throne, and removing God from his throne. That leads to disobeying God's commands, which are for our protection and help. As you assess your relationship, has being with this man resulted in you ignoring God and doing things your way? If you love Jesus less because of your boyfriend, and your life reflects this, that's a bad sign. Your relationship should be encouraging you both to love God and to follow him in everything. Is that true of your relationship?

What Do Those Around You Say about Your Relationship?

Often couples spend every possible hour with each other, and, as far as their friends are concerned, they've dropped off the planet. But dating should be a community affair, not an individualistic endeavor. If you haven't let others in on your relationship, then you need to. Get others involved so you don't have to sort through the hard things on your own, and so you don't have to make big decisions (like if you should get married) all by yourself. In regards to this relationship, what do your closest friends say? Are they supportive of your relationship, or have they expressed concerns? Sometimes single folks rely only on other single folks for advice. But please also check with married couples in your church. What do they say? Don't forget to find out what your parents think as well. They know you better than almost anyone else. Do they think your boyfriend is a good fit for you? Have you asked for advice from mature Christians? Godly wisdom comes from godly people. This could be a wise older couple in your church, or maybe your pastor or pastor's wife. All of this presumes that you have given your single friends, your parents, or fellow church members a chance to get to know your boyfriend. If they don't actually know him, how can they help you evaluate the relationship? Has your boyfriend made an effort to get to know the people who matter to you? The support of family, friends, and church for your relationship should give you confidence going forward. If you don't have that support, please pause and reconsider what their concerns might be.

What Does the Bible Say?

The Bible is more than a book. It's God's very own words, so it calls for a response from you. In every chapter of this book, I have referenced Scripture, showing what God thinks about passivity, pride, promiscuity, anger, control, etc. Do God's commands and principles matter to you? We come to know Christ through his Word, so the Word must matter for you in every area of your life, including how you evaluate your dating relationship. It's also vitally important that the Bible matters to your boyfriend. Does he care about God's Word? Do you read the Bible together? Do you talk about what you are learning and what the Spirit is teaching you? If your answer is "yes," then that is a wonderful foundation for your future. If the answer is "no," you should be very concerned about your relationship.

Are You Relying on Your Feelings?

When you are emotionally attached to someone, you will have a hard time letting go. But be careful not to evaluate your relationship based solely on your feelings. When faced with the question of whether or not to break up, is your only answer, "I love him, so I can't let go"? Is it that you *can't* let go, or that you *won't*? Emotional attachments are often strong, especially if you've engaged in premarital sex. Don't underestimate how much your feelings can cloud your judgment. As you try to stare out of the fog, notice how much all of the other important factors matter less. When your feelings are big and your emotional attachment is strong, God seems small. But he isn't small. He is your good Father. You can go to him and ask for help to make a hard choice, despite your strong feelings. He will help you!

Are You Driven by Fear?

How much are you motivated by your fears? Are you afraid you'll be alone for the rest of your life? Are you worried that you won't ever have children? Are you fearful that no one will take care of you when you are old? Do these fears motivate you to settle for the wrong man? The Bible has much to say to fearful people—all of it reassuring you that God is with you and for you (Psalms 46:1–3; 56:3–4; 1 Peter 3:5–7). Your fears are genuine, but there is something bigger than your fear in your life—it's the love of God (Romans 8:31–39). He is with you. He will not desert you. You are his dearly loved daughter.

Have You Prayed about Your Relationship?

When you pray, it's an admission that you need God's help and can't do this on your own. Don't make a decision about your relationship until you've sought the Lord. Talk to him. Confess your fears. Ask him to guide you. Tell him your joys and your disappointments. Tell him your hopes and your dreams. Tell him the things you are scared to tell anyone else. If you can't be honest with the One who made you, who can you be honest with?

Is Your Boyfriend Willing to Admit His Struggles
and Turn to God?

We all sin, so it's not a relationship deal breaker that your boyfriend has struggles. The important question is how is he handling those struggles? Is the passive man willing to get off the couch? Is the angry man willing to acknowledge and ask for help? Is the controlling man ready to relinquish control to God? Does your boyfriend recognize that his sins are first a problem between himself and God? Does he want to turn from his sin to God? If he is not willing to confess his sins to God and others, don't stay with him. Repentance is key to a good marriage; and deliberately choosing to marry an unrepentant man is a recipe for disaster.

Is Your Boyfriend Making Significant Changes in His Life?

Don't wait for your boyfriend to be less angry, less passive, or less controlling until after the marriage. If there is a pattern of sin in his life, his words matter less than his actions. Is he promising to make changes, or is he changing? You want to see the evidence of his willingness to fight his sin and to make positive changes *before* you tell him you'll marry him.

What Do You Want?

Behind every wise or foolish decision are goals and motivations that drive a person. Do you understand your goals and motivations? What resides within your heart? Get beyond the surface of your life, and dig into the deepest recesses of your heart. What do you think is making you hold on and is keeping you from letting go? What makes you queasy about the relationship? What scares you? What gives you hope? Who or what are you trusting? Do your goals reflect that you trust God or yourself more?

Are You Settling?

To settle is to decide to be with someone when you know God wants more for you. It's to choose the passive man, the immature Christian, the unteachable, the commitment-phobic, the unbelieving, the isolating, the promiscuous, the angry, or the controlling man, even though you know there is good reason not to. In any of the chapters where I listed why a woman settled, could you resonate with any of her reasons? Do you see yourself settling?

How to Break up for the Glory of God

Not every relationship ends in marriage. Though painful, breaking off a bad relationship is necessary to prevent future pain. Marrying the wrong guy leads to a difficult marriage and a hard life, so breaking up now, although painful, will not be as hard as a difficult marriage.

Sadly, Christians often act like everyone else when comes to splitting up. Couples ignore each other, plot revenge, gossip about each other, wrestle with bitterness, and continue fighting to get over the pain of the loss. They give way to anger, battle depression, or torture themselves by taking quick peeks at his or her social media accounts—*Has he moved on? Or is he still hurting just like me?* In the middle of a difficult breakup, it can be easy to start doubting God's goodness or to ditch church to avoid your ex.

The gospel of Jesus Christ makes a difference, even in the worst of moments. If Christian dating looks no different from the world, our faith has failed us. It shows itself to be useless. What would it look like to have a distinctly Christian breakup? What would it mean to break up for the glory of God? How do you end the relationship in a way that honors God and the other person, especially since he or she is a brother or sister in Christ?

There is no such thing as risk-free dating. Proverbs 13:12 (NIV) reminds us, "Hope deferred makes the heart sick, but a longing fulfilled is a tree of life." In a breakup there is usually at least one party who still hoped it would work out and suffers hope deferred. So be gentle and kind as you also share your honest concerns. Remember, for both of you, your hope is not in your relationship, but in God who never fails.

Here are some crucial things to remember that will help you live for God's glory even as you end your current relationship.[1]

"Let Your 'Yes' Be 'Yes' and Your 'No' Be 'No'" (Matthew 5:37)

Don't beat around the bush. If you know you need to break up, it's better to rip the bandage off and be straight-forward. Vagueness, ambiguity, or passive-aggressive games only lead to confusion and delay the end of the relationship. Be honest, but don't be mean or cruel. We are still called to speak the truth in love (Ephesians 4:15) and to speak only those words that build up and are fitting (Ephesians 4:29).

Talk in Person

This is a simple way to honor the other person and provide space for questions or discussion. Don't use texting, Twitter, Facebook, or any other form of social media to break up. Don't email or end the relationship over the phone. Technology can let you get out of a relationship without a face-to-face conversation. But that would not be kind. Don't take the easy way out; be willing to do the hard thing. Show your boyfriend the dignity that every image-bearer deserves by ending the relationship in person.

Don't Make the Breakup a One-Way Conversation

Often the person initiating the breakup has taken a great deal of time to reach his or her conclusions, so he or she shows up, unloads, and then leaves. Don't do that. Make the conversation a dialogue, not a monologue. Your desire to make it quick and painless will make you unload all your thoughts and then get out rather than stay and talk through it. There are times when it will be helpful to leave room for a follow-up conversation, then return to hear and process together a bit. The other person may have questions or things to discuss afterward. Some people are good thinking on their feet, and some aren't. Give the other person a chance to speak and ask questions.

Be Gracious, Loving, and Respectful in the Way You End It

The worst thing you can do is throw stones and cast blame on the other person, not only causing sadness over the lost relationship, but also provoking feelings of guilt, as if it is exclusively his or her fault. This is not

She's Got the Wrong Guy

the time to point out every little thing the other person did wrong during the relationship. *"You* did this . . ." or "One problem with *you* is . . ." or "I am not very attracted to *you* . . ." Every time you use the word "you" is probably a dart you are throwing at the person. Even in the act of breaking up, you need to be thoughtful, gracious, respectful, and loving toward the other person (Ephesians 4:1–3; Colossians 4:6; Titus 3:2). Keep a Christ-centered filter over your mouth. After all, he is a child of God, loved by God, so what gives you any right to treat him any differently than God does? If you are not sure how to do this, find an older, godly Christian man or woman and ask for help.

Make Thankfulness and Grace Your Goal

If your only goal is simply to end the relationship and then move on, your thinking is no different than a non-Christian. What about ending the relationship *and* also giving thanks to God for the time you had together (Psalm 86:12; 2 Thessalonians 1:3)? What about ending the relationship *and* talking to the person about the evidences of grace you see in them (James 4:6; 1 Corinthians 1:4)? Thankfulness and grace allow you to pave the way for a normal friendship that God might, in time, allow.

Don't let the termination of the relationship be your *only* goal. Often you are breaking up because you are focused on insurmountable problems or plenty of evidence of the other person's sins, but why not also find a way to spiritually encourage the person, even if the relationship was hard?

Be Thoughtful about Where You Break Up

Pick a location that is conducive to having a hard conversation.[2] Someplace that is discrete and probably private is wise. Having a hard conversation in public is not a great idea, especially if the other person becomes emotional.

Be Careful about When You Break Up

Don't go out on a romantic date and *then* break up.[3] Timing is key. "A word fitly spoken is like apples of gold in settings of silver" (Proverbs 25:11). An apple of gold is valuable. An apple of gold in a setting of silver is even more valuable. So also are wise words given at the right time (Proverbs 15:23). The worth of those words is invaluable if you time things right. Here's my advice—if you know you are ready to end the relationship, be swift about it. Get it done as soon as possible, but be sensitive about when you do it.

Don't Use the Advice of a Pastor, Close Friend, Parent,
or Counselor as an Excuse

"I talked to X about this, and he or she thinks we should break up."
It's tempting to do this rather than taking responsibility yourself. When
it comes to deciding who we will or won't marry, we need to take advice.
Yet remember that ultimately this is a decision each person must make. If
you agree with the counsel you are receiving, own it. Don't use someone
else's advice as justification for the decision and a way to prove that you are
making the right decision.

Fight against Bitterness (Hebrews 12:15)

When our hope for the relationship is shattered, it is tempting to play
the details over and over in our minds until they fester. What can we do
to fight against bitterness? How can we stop it from taking root in our
hearts? For an answer, take a look at the next three sections.

There Is No Failure in Ending the Relationship

Remember it isn't a "fail" if you decide to end the relationship. That
was the purpose of dating—to see if this friendship might lead to marriage. But if you have clear reasons why it would be *bad* for you to get
married (or at least, as best you can tell, it would be *unwise*), then ending
the relationship, especially if you conclude it graciously and lovingly, can
be considered a "success."

Assume the Best in the Other Person's Motives

We read in 1 Corinthians 13:7 that love "believes all things, hopes all
things, endures all things." We can't peer into others' hearts, judge their
motives, and conclude that they were being malicious in the ways they
handled the relationship. Our sinful nature presses us to believe the worst
about your boyfriend's motives. Is there a way in which God can help you
to assume the best in them?

Preach Truth to Yourself (as in Psalms 42:5; 62:5)

When you struggle with the temptation toward bitterness, you can
let go of those feelings because God is righteous and just. We don't need
to take vengeance into our own hands. Paul writes in Romans 12:19, 21,
"Do not take revenge, my friends, but leave room for God's wrath, for it
is written: 'It is mine to avenge; I will repay,' says the Lord. . . . Do not
be overcome by evil, but overcome evil with good." Revenge belongs to
God, not to us. The Christian's responsibility is to forgive for the wrong

done. We can forgive by remembering how God has forgiven us in Christ, as we see in Ephesians 4:32, "Be kind and compassionate to one another, forgiving each other, just as in Christ God forgave you."

Find Your Identity in Christ, Not in the Lost Relationship

"I am still confident of this: I will see the goodness of the LORD in the land of the living. Wait for the LORD; be strong and take heart and wait for the LORD" (Psalm 27:13–14 NIV). Just as you find your identity in Christ during the dating relationship, so, too, this broken relationship does not define you. Most of your friends or fellow church members are not thinking about it as much as you are, so when people ask how your life is, feel free to share other things. Be careful in how you share details about breakup, especially if you're struggling to build up the other person in your speech (Ephesians 4:29).

Remember Your Responsibility to Do Good to All Christians

It's okay after the breakup to distance yourself or to set some boundaries in order to protect your heart—give it some time to heal. Don't hang out. Don't email or text one another for a while. Make it a clean break. On the other hand, you have a responsibility to do good to your boyfriend as your Christian brother. Paul says in Colossians 3:13 (NIV), "Bear with each other and forgive whatever grievances you may have against one another. Forgive as the Lord forgave you." This includes a former boyfriend, especially if yours is the broken heart in the aftermath of the breakup.

Don't Assume That You Must Go to Another Church

It is possible to stay in the same church with the person you once dated. Too many people assume that they must leave because of how uncomfortable it is initially. It's easier to run and avoid than to do the hard work of living "at peace" with one another (Romans 12:18), and eventually again being friends. It is not wrong to go to another church, but we don't want to presume that is the only thing you can do after a breakup.

Your Grief Will Pass

As with anything that is hard, many will experience some sense of grief over the end of the relationship. Grief is a sign that you are sad about the lost relationship, and also about the lost dreams and hopes for a future together. Grief after a breakup is normal if the relationship was meaningful to you. Sadness, crying, and mixed emotions are to be expected right after the breakup. But, with time, the dark clouds will part and the sun will come out again. God shows grace and comfort in the midst of the grief over a lost relationship.

God Is Sanctifying You

Regardless of how painful the breakup, God is using this difficult experience to sanctify you. Paul says in Romans 8:28, "And we know that in all things God works for the good of those who love him, who have been called according to his purpose." Your breakup is included in this phrase "all things." If you are a Christian, God is using this experience for your good. As hard as this is, he is making you more like his Son. You might not want that comfort right now. With the pain and sorrow over the lost relationship, you might just want to be with your ex-boyfriend. Or you might want to just wallow in your hurt or sadness. But take comfort from the fact that God wants to use this anguish to refine you, using trials "of various kinds" (James 1:2) to help you become more like Christ.

Moving On

Breaking up is hard to do, but it's necessary if you are dating the wrong guy. Trust God in this. Don't give in to the temptation to go at it your own way. If breaking up is the right thing to do, then do it, and be distinctly Christian in how you do it.

The story doesn't end here. Having ended the relationship, you are free again to date someone. To find genuine godliness in a man is like a hungry sheep rounding the corner to find green fields and lush pastures. That's our next chapter—the pursuit of a real Christian man (chapter 16).

16

In Pursuit of a Real Christian Man

When you think of your future husband, what do you imagine? What immediately comes to mind? Consider a few options:

A. A rich businessman, who can give everything you materially want.
B. A tall, good-looking, well-built athletic man.
C. A good talker, someone who will have deep and meaningful conversations with you.
D. A really funny guy, who is energetic and outgoing.
E. _____ (You fill in the blank. What's your ideal?)
F. A genuine Christian man, who seeks to love you just as Christ loves the church.

How does the Christian man stack up against the other options? In this chapter, we want to consider what matters to you in your quest for a husband. While there are good aspects to each of the options listed above (e.g., a guy should provide, work at communication, etc.), a man who is servant-hearted, faithful, and strong in his faith *should* be of utmost importance to you.

Margaret and Anthony

Margaret found herself struggling with a decision. She had been dating Anthony for months, but now the relationship was getting serious. Even though she had been a Christian for a while, studied her Bible, went to church, and cultivated relationships with Christian friends, she still struggled with *whom* she should marry. Anthony was a growing Christian. He had made mistakes along the way, but he was earnestly trying to figure out how to lead her well, and how to date as a Christian. Anthony was a bit nerdy and more introverted than she had hoped for. When Margaret thought of her future husband, she imagined someone who was outgoing and the life of the party. Would she stay with this nerdy Christian guy, or would she hold out for someone different?

Like Margaret, you might wrestle with what the world around you values in a guy, and those qualities look shiny and nice to you, like new jewelry or a watch unwrapped on Christmas morning. Here's the thing, however: *every Christian woman needs to value what God values.*

What do you want in a life partner? A good-looking, well-built man? A guy who is always the life of the party? A man who works at a well-respected job—a lawyer or a doctor—or at least has the potential to make a ton of money? A chap who will one day be famous? The most popular guy in school—the quarterback of the football team or the lead singer in the band? Don't be distracted by qualities that are less valuable than a man's character.

- If a guy is good at telling jokes at a party, but is a jerk as a dad, it doesn't matter that he is the life of the party.
- If the guy is good-looking, but is lazy about work, his good looks won't put a roof over your head or food on the table, especially when children enter the picture.
- If a guy shows you a lot of attention, says kind things to you, and yet, also has a foul mouth or is controlling, he's no good for you. Eventually, he'll curse at you and micromanage your life.
- If a guy is a good athlete, or a good kisser, or popular with your friends, but doesn't know how to prioritize your needs, or sacrifice for you, it doesn't matter what he accomplishes.

Let me describe this a different way—maybe he is nerdy, or not as outgoing as you wanted, or not as well-built as you hoped, or not as attractive as you thought, but he loves Jesus, he's gracious, patient, and humble, and he's deeply committed to you. Would that be enough for you? Pause and think about it for a moment. What do you value in a man? What *really* matters to you? What matters to the world should be secondary to what matters to God. *Put first things first, and second things second. Make God's values your priority in your quest for a man.*

Robertson and Muriel

Sometimes life holds surprises. Muriel was vibrant, creative, and articulate.[1] She painted a portrait for the former President of Columbia

Bible College and Seminary. It was so well done that the trustees commissioned her to do a painting of her husband, Robertson McQuilkin, who served as the most recent President of Columbia Bible. She had a radio program called "Listen Up" geared to women, but it was so thoughtful that many businessmen also tuned in for daily encouragement. WMHK's station manager, the program manager, and the producer started talking about national syndication. Opportunities to speak at conferences and other events abounded, and she had a vibrant public ministry just like her husband, Robertson. She was just as gifted at home. She delighted in cooking, hosting, and entertaining many in their home, and for her it wasn't a burden—just a normal part of their ministry to a growing college and seminary community.

The first sign of a potential problem came when she repeated a story she had told just five minutes prior. Robertson "reminded her that this was a rerun. She just laughed and continued. *Funny*, [he] thought, *that's never happened before.*[2] From then on, it occasionally did. Little did they know what lay ahead.

Several years later, Muriel was undergoing tests for her heart when a young doctor mentioned to Robertson, "You may need to think about the possibility of Alzheimer's." Denial is a common first reaction. Robertson was dumbfounded at the doctor's comment, *These young doctors are so presumptuous—and insensitive.*[3] But was it presumptuous? What began was a slow descent into oblivion, with each part of Muriel's ministry stripped away.

Planning menus became increasing difficult, so they stopped entertaining.

The portrait of Robertson was too hard to finish.

One day Robertson was summoned to the radio station, where the three executives tried to explain their plight in a polite way, but didn't know how to say what they needed to say. Robertson relieved the tension with a simple question, "Are you meeting with me to tell us that Muriel can't continue?" From the expression in their faces, it was clear that was the case. No national syndication; her radio ministry was done.

Muriel refused to give up. She continued to accept speaking invitations, only to come home crushed and frustrated, as she frequently lost her train of thought and things went poorly. Eventually she came to face the painful reality—she had to give up her public ministry.

A neurologist confirmed Robertson's worst fears. She had Alzheimer's. They sought a second opinion at Duke University Medical Center— "the doctor asked her to name the Gospels, and [Muriel] looked pleadingly at [Robertson] for help."[4] His heart sank. What should have been obvious was not. She didn't know the answer.

Muriel occasionally pondered after Alzheimer's was mentioned on television, "I wonder if I will ever have that?"[5] Robertson witnessed the slow death of the woman he had known and loved for four decades. The articulate, creative, energetic, vibrant wife he had married faded away.

Over the next two years, it became harder for Robertson to leave Muriel for the day, let alone go on ministry trips. Being apart grew increasingly difficult. The trustees of the school made arrangements for someone to stay with Muriel during the day. As he headed out to school, Muriel would panic, and in her own determined way, would follow him to the office, showing up as much as ten times a day. One night, as he undressed her and got her ready for bed, he found bloodied feet. Muriel's affection for her husband was shown in her repeated trips to his office, which mattered much more than the injuries she obtained on her trips. "Such love," the doctor said at her next appointment. A moment later, the doctor added: "I have a theory that characteristics developed across years come out at moments like these."

At fifty-seven years of age, Robertson had hoped to hold out until retirement at sixty-five, but that didn't seem possible. Trusted, lifelong friends, and many godly people, encouraged him to put her in a nursing home and continue his ministry. Those who didn't know Robertson well would ask, "Shouldn't you put God first?" You can just imagine the wide-range of comments and suggestions, like "Why not put her in a nursing home? She barely even knows you."

Though leaving the ministry was painful, the choice was obvious to Robertson. It was a matter of integrity for him. Many years earlier, he had promised Muriel, "in sickness and in health . . . till death us do part." As he resigned, he reflected on the reason he needed to leave his job to care for Muriel:

> It was only fair. She had, after all, cared for me for almost four decades with marvelous devotion; now it was my turn . . . if I took care of her for forty years, I would never be out of her debt.[6]

There was a marvelous outpouring of appreciation after his decision was made. Pastors told their story. Couples renewed their vows. *Christianity Today* asked him to write up their story for publication. The response was a mystery to him, until one day a doctor explained, "Almost all women stand by their men; but few men stand by their women." Now it made sense. Though his choice was consistent with the vows he took four decades earlier, Robertson's devoted response was uncommon among men in general.

I would argue a Christian man *can* and *should* demonstrate this kind of integrity and self-sacrifice for his wife. It's a natural extension of his trust in Christ. So when you look for a man, find one who is willing to give up his life for his wife, just as Robertson did for Muriel, and more importantly, as Christ did for his bride, the church (Ephesians 5:21–33).

There Is No Such Thing as a Perfect Man

You might be thinking, *Where do I find such a man?* As far as you're concerned, the guys who live like this are probably already married. But they are out there. I know some of them myself. And in my years as a pastor I have consistently seen godly men overlooked by women because of superficial, non-essential things, like their physical appearance or age or charisma.

You can't expect a twenty-year-old man, or even a thirty-year-old, to have the same kind of wisdom, maturity, and experience. I know very few twenty-five-year-olds with the maturity to make the same decision as Robertson McQuilkin did in caring for Muriel.

Where does that leave you? How should you respond to a boyfriend who sins and sometimes does unhelpful things? Show grace in response to a man's immaturity, weaknesses, and mistakes. Every man will need time to grow up in his faith, and one of the primary ways he will grow in faith is by spending time with you.

Distinguish between a guy who is committed to Christ and earnestly desires to grow, but is immature in some of his decisions, and a more problematic man who is characterized by anger, or pride, or laziness, or passivity, or isolation, or unbelief, or control. These are two completely different kinds of men. Some men have sin patterns that make them unworthy of being a husband, until the Lord humbles them and they see their need for Christ.

Choose wisely. The imperfect guy—the one who is growing in Christ and still has growing to do as he figures out how to be a boyfriend and a husband—give him a chance. Ditch the problematic man. Stay away from him.

No matter who you marry, he won't be perfect. Janelle certainly thought her boyfriend would be. In facing the reality that her boyfriend, and soon-to-be fiancé, is a sinner, and not perfect like a Disney prince, she said to me: "I didn't think the man I would marry would be perfect, but I assumed he'd be pretty close."

Don't compromise on your choice of a possible husband. Don't settle for a man who is far from God and shows no signs of change. But give the imperfect man who loves Christ a chance. Trust God in what he values. Choose what matters to God. Let his values be shown in your choice of a husband.

17
Why Waiting Is Okay

Waiting is not a word most of us like. People today *hate* to wait. Amazon is late with my package, yet again. And I want it right now. I stand in line at Chick-Fil-A for a few minutes and think, *They need to speed this up. I've got things to do.* I hover around my microwave as my food warms up. It's only a minute, but it still feels too long. I send an email or a text, and I get annoyed if the person doesn't get back to me right away. A friend asks me, "Did you get my text?" which really means, "Why didn't you answer? What's taking you so long?"

See what the culture has done to us? It says to us, "Why the delay? Go get what you want right now." Waiting in line is bad. Waiting for your food is bad. Waiting to hear back from someone is bad. Bad, bad, bad.

If you are single, you hope to get married and have children. You want the kind of future that you see many of your friends already starting. Every time a friend announces her engagement, every time you sit at a wedding by yourself, every time you are home alone on a Friday night, every time a close friend tells you she is pregnant, it's easy for you to think waiting is bad. You might wonder: *Why keep waiting for the right guy to show up? Life is passing by. Why not take things into my own hands?*

Why is waiting okay? I'd suggest that waiting is not bad, but in fact, in the kingdom of God, waiting is redemptive and good. It's hard, painful, and even annoying to wait for what we want, but just because something is frustrating doesn't mean it is bad for us.

The basic posture of the Christian life is one of waiting.[1] To understand what this means, I want to tackle two questions—*Why is waiting so hard?* Delay is painful and exasperating at times. No denying that, but what makes it this way? And as a Christian, *how do I wait well?* If waiting is a fundamental part of what it means to be a Christian, how do we wait in a way that honors God, demonstrates patience and wisdom, and allows us to be a good witness to those who are watching?

Why Is Waiting So Hard?

Let me mention six reasons why waiting for a good relationship is so difficult, and many days painful—singleness, happiness, heart exposure, delayed gratification, impatience, and desires for sex.

Singleness

In many churches today, singleness is not seen as a beautiful thing. To many singles, it feels more like a disease that needs to be cured. Who wants to be single? Even worse, who wants to *stay* single? Marriage is talked about in spectacular terms, and rightly so, because the Bible has a high view of marriage. But an aftershock of all this conversation about marriage is that singles are made to feel like second-class citizens in the kingdom of God. Married people talk about facing their selfishness in ways that they never experienced in singleness. Or they talk about the joy of companionship, and how their marital relationship is a portrait of the gospel. All of this is true, but it leaves a single to think, *Am I somehow incomplete if I am not married? Is there something wrong with me if I don't get married?*

Let's admit upfront that there is hurt, grief, and vulnerability in your singleness. Loneliness is painful. Who wants to be home alone again on a Friday or Saturday night? Who wants to go grocery shopping and cook for just one person? Who hasn't felt uncomfortable when an aunt or uncle inquires, "Haven't met anyone yet?" Who hasn't felt the mixture of joy and sadness when a friend or sister gives birth to another baby? Who wants to carry the burden of provision or have to make all of the decisions on your own?

Prolonged singleness—singleness that goes on for years—makes the burden feel heavier. It's so easy to think, "If I had just gotten married young, I might not even know this burden was there. So why, God? Why do I have to carry this burden?"

Happiness

Your parents, teachers, coaches, and culture confidently declare, "You *deserve* to be happy." They treat happiness as a basic right of humanity. You begin to think that God owes you as much of happiness as you can get.

Stephanie captured a single woman's frustrations with waiting:

> Waiting isn't easy because the enemy would have you believe that you are being denied the one thing that would make you happy.

If only you had a husband, you would be happy. If only you had children, you would be happy. If only you had a nicer house, a better car. If only you had the one thing, you can fill in the blank with anything, you would be happy. Life would be easier. You would be satisfied. It's why they don't tell you what happens after the prince and princess get together in the fairytale, because you would never find real life as satisfying as the mystery.[2]

You can fill your life with good things now, but will that really be satisfying? Will a husband give you ultimate joy? If you had children, would you be truly content? If you got to leave the single life behind, would you think more highly of yourself? If you fill your life with a husband, children, and house, would you be pleased? Sadly, we are far too often focused on what we can get for ourselves right now. We entertain ourselves with an endless stream of happy things. We don't often focus on investing into eternal treasures, nor do we long for them. Rather, we contemplate: *How do I get what I want?* or *What do I do when my desires and dreams don't work out?* We know Jesus's words about storing up treasure in heaven (Matthew 6:19–21), but tangible treasures seem so much more appealing right now.

Life does not go well when you make earthly things your hope and treasure. When you look for your ultimate happiness in a husband, children, a beautiful home, or a wonderful life now, you'll be disappointed, anxious, confused, or even hurt, because none of these things are meant to carry the weight of your ultimate hopes. Putting your hope in earthly treasures shows that you are not letting your heart rest in satisfaction with the Lord. An already hard life is made harder when your desire for happiness takes center stage in your life.

Heart Exposure

Waiting is a powerful tool in the hands of God because it reveals our hearts. God puts us through difficult seasons and delays his promises to us because he wants to expose our heart motives and unbelief. When you struggle, or are confused, disappointed, frustrated, or anxious, your heart is uncovered.

Your heart cries, "I want a husband" (a good desire), but if you drilled down deeper as you waited on the Lord's timing, what would you see? Is it possible that your desire has changed to "Lord, I *need* a husband"? From there, it's easy to demand, "Lord, you *owe* me a husband." You might buy into the notion that because you've been faithful on your part to go to church, read the Bible, and go to Bible studies, God needs to give you what you want in return. You expect the quid pro quo, and if you don't get it, you might believe, *I must be worthless if no one wants to love me.* You start to equate the waiting period with something being wrong with you, or thinking that God made a mistake when he made you. You believe the lie that you've got too many faults for someone to actually love you. Having to wait means you must be unlovable.

Rarely would anyone explicitly say these things—"Lord, I need a husband," or "Lord, you owe me," or "I must be worthless if no one wants to love me." What comes out of your mouth is the good desire of "I want a husband," but look closely at what lurks in the depths of your heart. As your good desires are put on hold, your heart is exposed for you and God to see more clearly. Waiting is difficult because it shows what you really worship.

Delayed Gratification

Have you ever seen a kid staring into a cookie jar? You hear her lips smacking, and her eyes glare at the chocolate cookie with unusual focus. Mother says, "You've got to wait until after dinner. You can't have one right now." Yet, her heart says, "Ugh. I want one right now. Why does Mommy make me wait?" As soon as you tell her she can't have it, she wants it even more. She craves it. She longs for it.

Waiting is difficult because we forfeit instant gratification. We don't get to satisfy our desires immediately, which is highly unusual in our day and age. We live in a world where instant satisfaction is the norm—whether that is movies-on-demand or groceries showing up at our doorstep in minutes. We hate to wait because waiting denies desires that we think will bring us happiness.

Solomon made a wise observation—"A hope deferred makes the heart sick, but a desire fulfilled is a tree of life" (Proverbs 13:12). Delayed fulfillment is hard because it leads to frustration, disappointment, and sadness. Every day you have to wait for a man, a child, or a house, you second-guess God. But when he provides, you think, *My life is wonderful. I've finally arrived! God must love me!*

Waiting is hard because the unknown is hard. You're draped in uncertainty. It is agonizing because you don't know when it will end. Some days you wonder if your singleness will ever end. If you knew that you would be married five years from now, then you think you could actually enjoy this time of singleness. But you just don't know. God doesn't tell you that kind of thing.

Waiting is challenging because you don't know *if* it will end. You are not promised a husband. You have a very strong desire for a husband, companionship, and someone to share your life. Perhaps you cringe when you meet older single women. It's easy to make your prayer, "Lord, don't let that be me."

Apparent Passivity

Just like waiting, passivity is a negative word. If there is something you can do about a problem, then you should do it, right? Flirt with the guy, so he knows you're interested. Don't just wait around. If you wait for him to initiate, or show interest, it might never happen. If you wait around, he might find someone else. Waiting is hard because on the surface of things it looks like you are passive. You fret that you're letting life drift by. You feel like you're not tackling the problem.

It feels like waiting is a wasteful exercise in passivity. And it's hard because you don't want life to pass you by, and you don't want to simply be tossed around by life's circumstances. Waiting is hard because you wonder if you're missing an opportunity to change your situation.

Impatience

It's easy for impatience to get the best of you. You are eager to start your dreams, and annoyed at God for making you wait. You know impatience is a problem—it's not a fruit of the Spirit; it's not commended in Scripture. But active submission to God's timing is hard. You want your dreams fulfilled much sooner than God does.

Impatience is fueled by troubling questions—will God give me what I want? Will he answer my prayers? Will I ever get to be happy? Will I be stuck with singleness for the rest of my life?

Impatience prevents you from believing that what God has given you today is best, and that your good desire or dreams are not God's plan for you right now. Is it possible that you are hoping for the right things, but according to God, it might be the wrong time?[3]

Desires for Sex

Sex is too often exclusively portrayed as a male interest. The books on lust, internet pornography, or masturbation center around men, not women. And yet, women have sex drives too. It's not just a male interest—women want to have sex too.

In our over-sexualized culture, waiting for sex is particularly hard because everyone around you is doing it. You wait because of your love for Christ, but you get questioned and sometimes mocked if you are honest with your non-Christian friends. The pressure to conform to the culture is unending, and the sexual temptations grow ever stronger. Fighting sexual temptations in a season of singleness is hard; battling them in prolonged singleness many days feels like cruel torture from God.

Waiting is also hard because women want to have children. Sex produces babies. Yes, sex provides intimacy and pleasure, but a fundamental reason why God gave us sex is for procreation. A woman can feel her biological clock ticking as she gets older. After thirty-five, medical professionals warn that the risk of potential problems in pregnancy grows with each passing year. If you don't have children, you can feel useless. As one fifty-year-old miserably proclaimed, "I have a body part that won't ever function that way."

How Do I Wait Well?

There are plenty of reasons why waiting makes the Christian life challenging. But, with eyes focused on the cross, let's shift to how Christians can wait well. Frustration, anxiety, fear, disappointment, anger, confusion—these things don't need to define you. It is possible to have genuine joy as you wait on the Lord. The question is *how*?

Remember Your Singleness Uniquely Displays the Gospel

The apostle Paul talks about how marriage is a beautiful display of the gospel in Ephesians 5:22–33.[4] Just as Christ gave up his life for the church, so also the husband should give over his life for his bride. And just as the church is called to follow Christ, so also wives should follow their husbands.

But where does that leave single adults? If you are not married, you don't display the gospel in the same way that married people do. Rather, you have the privilege of displaying the gospel in a way that is uniquely possible because of your singleness. Paul writes about this in 1 Corinthians 7:

> I would like you to be free from concern. An unmarried man is concerned about the Lord's affairs—how he can please the Lord. But a married man is concerned about the affairs of

this world—how he can please his wife—and his interests are divided. An unmarried woman or virgin is concerned about the Lord's affairs: Her aim is to be devoted to the Lord in both body and spirit. But a married woman is concerned about the affairs of this world—how she can please her husband. I am saying this for your own good, not to restrict you, but that you may live in a right way in undivided devotion to the Lord. (vv. 32–35 NIV)

Paul says your main goal as a Christian single is to live your life in single-minded devotion to the Lord (v. 35). Singles have an advantage over married people because their interests are not divided (v. 34). A married woman is concerned with the affairs of this world—how she can please her spouse, how to care for her children, how to provide for her family—while a single woman has the freedom to uniquely focus on the Lord's affairs (vv. 32–35). Married people can't do this. They can't show a single-minded devotion to the Lord, because inherent in marriage is responsibility for a spouse and children.

Marriage is temporal and only singleness extends into heaven. Have you ever thought about that? That's what Jesus argued as he talked with the Sadducees, in Matthew 22. He said no one will be married or given to marriage in heaven. We'll all be single, and the only thing that will matter is our relationship to Christ.

Wait on God

Waiting for God is not like standing at a Burger King counter waiting for your food. Our ability to wait as Christians depends not on *what* we wait for (like a burger), but *who* we wait for—God himself.

The ease of waiting depends on who, what, or where we place our hope. The psalmist writes:

> Our soul waits for the LORD,
> he is our help and our shield,
> For our heart is glad in him,
> because we trust in his holy name. (Psalm 33:20–21)

We wait on God himself. He is our help and shield. We can wait gladly for his promises to be fulfilled because we trust in him. If we trust that God is good and that he has good intended for us in our waiting, then it makes the delays more bearable. Or even better, it makes it possible to find joy in the waiting. It may seem strange for God to be called a helper, but that's exactly what the verses say. He is "our help." The Lord of the universe helps us to gladly persevere in waiting. We don't have to be afraid of waiting because we know the arc of the Lord's faithfulness is long.[5] Rather than waiting for a man, a baby, a job or a house (all of which are uncertain), we wait on someone who is always certain. We wait on God himself. Our joy in waiting is a testimony to this fallen world that we trust ultimately in God, and not in this world.

In this same vein, Becca commented to me:

> "Psalm 27:14 says to 'be strong and take heart and wait for the Lord.' It doesn't say to wait for the date, or wait for the job, or wait for a specific outcome to any situation. It says to wait *for the Lord*—for him and not for the good gifts that he gives. Isaiah 49:23 says, '[T]hose who wait for me shall not be put to shame.' We are *fools* if we wait for anyone else. When the object of my waiting is misplaced, anxiety, discontent, tears and doubt often follow."[6]

Psalm 130:5–6 says,

> I wait for the LORD, my soul waits,
> and in his word I hope;
> my soul waits for the Lord,
> more than watchmen for the morning,
> more than watchman for the morning.

You can wait because like the psalmist, you can put your hope in God's Word. God has revealed himself in his Word. The psalmist hopes in God's Word because it is there he will meet God, and grow in his relationship with God. The Word itself promises the psalmist (and you) more of God.

In v. 6, the psalmist repeats the statement—"my souls waits for the Lord *more than* watchmen for the morning, *more than* watchmen for the morning." Poetry repeats a phrase in order to emphasize it, like highlighting an important line. The watchmen who stays up all night *yearns* for the morning to come, but the psalmist yearns for God *even more*.

As you wait on God, believe that he is good and that he intends good for you. In those moments when you feel like you can wait no longer, and you question his goodness, remember that his goodness was demonstrated through the cross.

Can God be any less good to me on the average Tuesday morning than he was on that monumental Friday afternoon when he hung on a cross in my place? The answer is a resounding NO. God will not be less good to me tomorrow either, because God *cannot* be less good to me.[7]

God is the giver of good gifts (James 1:17; Luke 11:11–13). Trusting in his goodness makes it possible for us to wait on him.

Share Your Heartache and Pain with Others

The Bible is realistic about how hard waiting is. Your pain is real, so you don't have to fake it. Whoever coined the cliché "fake it until you make it" must not have realized that's a dumb way to approach life. Be honest with others who are called to carry your burdens. Lean in on your friends. "A friend loves at all times, and a brother is born for adversity" (Proverbs 17:17).

You don't have to wait alone. In fact, let me say this more strongly— *you can't wait alone.* A church community is essential for your survival. You need a church community that values your singleness, and at the same time, fosters a culture where singles equally value marriage. It's necessary for a church's health to have singleness and marriage thrive together, side-by-side, acting as essential components of that same community.

We gather on Sundays at church to help each other wait. Because, of course, we are all (both married and single) waiting for something. Local churches are *waiting co-operatives*. We explore the goodness of God in his Word and share it with each other. We hear testimonies of God's faithfulness, which help us to wait. We remind one another that this world is not our home. We cry on each other's shoulders. We pray waiting prayers and sing songs that remind us to wait. We confess our sins. As long as we are in this world, we wait.

Be Patient

Patience is our ability to lovingly endure when God's promises are not yet fulfilled. You are naturally impatient, but God teaches you to faithfully persevere. The fruit of patient waiting is goodness and kindness.

God is faithful, but he also takes his time to work out his purposes in our lives. As God works through his own timing, we're called to remain vigilant, sober-minded, prayerful, and watchful (Colossians 4:2; 1 Peter 4:7; Psalm 5:1–3). God will fulfill his Word and show himself faithful. When we short-circuit waiting on God, we rush to fill our lives with everything we feel God has neglected to provide. We don't wait. We control, manipulate, cajole, argue, complain, covet, and grumble (James 4:1–3), all with the hope of getting what we want. But in this, we show that we trust ourselves more than we trust the Lord. It's like knocking on someone's door and walking away, or making a phone call but hanging up before they answer. It makes no sense. God will finish what he started. God will show himself to be faithful to his promises, so Christian—wait and be patient. Go to the door, knock, and wait for God to answer.

One of the hardest areas to show patience is in the area of sex. Sexual temptation plagues you. The culture screams in your ear, "Get it now! It feels so good! Don't delay!" God has made sex a beautiful thing, and he asks you to entrust your sex drive to him. Sex is more than just pleasure and having kids. It's powerful and most people underestimate its influence. God has reserved sex for marriage because he knows what's best for you. Handling sex before marriage is like messing with dynamite. Most singles don't realize (when they first engage in extramarital sex) its potential to destroy their life. So God asks you to be patient and wait.

Remember Jesus Is Worth It

Keep your gaze on Christ because he is worth it. Philippians 3:20–21 says: "But our citizenship is in heaven, and from it we *await a Savior*, the Lord Jesus Christ, who will transform our lowly body to be like his glorious body, by the power that enables him even to subject all things to himself" (emphasis added).

Disney wants you to believe that you are waiting for Prince Charming, who will swoop in on a white horse, fulfilling your every last dream. God says you are really awaiting the Prince of Peace. So as you wait, remember *who* it is you are waiting for. Christ beckons you to long for things that don't pass away, things that are eternal, certain, proven, and stable. He teaches you to wait for the real thing—himself.

While you wait, Christ will meet you in the midst of your pain, vulnerability, and loneliness. The warmth, comfort, and love of your risen Savior can draw even the most impatient or unhappy woman to himself.

Some days, in reading your Bible, the truth feels "cold." "Cold" comfort is hard to bear. It's easy to think, *I'd rather have the warmth of a man's embrace than the cold truth.* Even if the truth feels chilly, remember the Bible is still the only reliable pathway to deep fellowship with God.

A bad marriage is not better than struggling through singleness. For many women I know, the problem isn't so much convincing them that it's better to choose the right guy than the wrong guy. Often there doesn't seem to be a "right guy" around. The problem is convincing them that it's better to be *single* than spend their life with the wrong guy. So that sends us racing back to a few pivotal questions—Is Christ enough for you? Can he be all that you need? Can you build your entire life around him?

Waiting does draw you near to your Savior. God uses these periods of waiting to strip your superficial layers and dig down to the core of your heart. Orient your life around Jesus. *Commit yourself this day to choosing Christ first—over any relationship.* You can't lose if you build your life on him. He's the solid rock (Psalm 18:2), the refuge (Psalms 5:11; 7:1; 57:1), the sure foundation (Matthew 7:24–27), and the everlasting hope (1 Timothy 4:10) on which you can rely.

Actively Wait

When our desires are denied, we can slip into passive resignation—just slogging through life with a defeated outlook. But a Christian can't passively wait. It is just not possible. This will sound like an oxymoron, but a Christian can only *actively* wait. This is the paradox of the Christian life. As sons and daughters of God, we wait for his promises to be fulfilled. Waiting is what we do because we worship a God whose plans take time.[8] We know God will honor his promises; he will fulfill what he has said to us. We know this because of what he has already done for us through Christ. The Cross is our guarantee that we are not waiting in vain, though many days it feels like that's what we are doing.

Active waiting means trusting God rather than giving way to fear or worry (Psalm 56; Matthew 6:19–33). It means choosing patience instead of wallowing in impatience (Psalms 37:7; 40:1; Proverbs 25:15). It means fighting for purity rather than giving yourself over to sexual temptation and lust (Matthew 5:8, 27–30). It means engaging in community instead of fighting on your own (Hebrews 10:24–25; Proverbs 18:1). And most importantly, it means cherishing Christ rather than cultivating your selfish desires (2 Corinthians 5:15).

A fundamental part of waiting as a Christian is learning to bear up under uncertainty (to steal a phrase from Elizabeth Elliot). You don't know if or when the unknowns will end, but you choose to walk by faith, keeping your eyes set on the next thing, and standing in the shadow of the Cross.

Adopt a Long-Term View

Don't be shortsighted. To focus exclusively on a husband, children, and a full home, you limit your vision to that which you can only find here on earth. No man will ever fulfill your ultimate desires. There is only one groom who can give you what you most deeply need.

As you wait now, and experience delays in your dreams, and wrestle with God's goodness and faithfulness, remember that you are married to Christ (2 Corinthians 11:1–3). He's the only bridegroom who knows what you need. He invites you to a wedding feast on the last day, where you will be the bride of Christ (Revelation 19:6–8). And this is a wedding reception you won't have to plan, because Christ is planning it for you.

Isaiah spoke about this final wedding banquet:

On this mountain the LORD of hosts will make for all peoples a feast of rich food, a feast of well-aged wine, of rich food full of marrow, of aged wine well refined. . . . He will swallow up death forever; and the Lord GOD will wipe away tears from all faces, and the reproach of his people he will take away from all the earth, for the LORD has spoken. *It will be said on that day, "Behold, this is our God: we have waited for him, that he might save us. This is the LORD; we have waited for him; let us be glad and rejoice in his salvation."* (Isaiah 25:6, 8–9, emphasis added)

The prophet speaks about the consummation of all things. He looks forward to the end of the story, the final days after Christ has returned in all of his glory, when the wedding banquet has begun and death is swallowed up forever.

Pastor and author Bobby Jamieson declares:

We don't have full satisfaction now. If you trust in Christ you are on the guest list for the greatest party in history. Everything else is just appetizers. No earthly pleasure can give you all you want. If you fill up on them, you'll ruin your appetite for the feast to come. We can go without now because we know what is coming.[9]

No earthly pleasure can give you all you want. On that last day, Christ will fully and finally satisfy you. Don't be deceived by the sweetness of inferior appetizers, when, in fact, nothing can compare to the delight we'll find with Christ.

The striking thing about the Isaiah passage is that it marks the end of waiting. On that last day, you'll be able to say all the waiting was worth it. God will have fulfilled all his promises. His faithfulness will be proven true. And in response, we'll rejoice and sing a hymn of victory: "This is God; he has saved us. We have waited for him, but we wait no longer!" As pastor Jamieson has said, "On that day, there will be no more faith, only soul-satisfying sight. There will be no more struggle against sin; no more failure, only freedom to do God's will; no more pain, only peace; no more sickness, only strength; no more loss, only the all-satisfying presence of God."[10]

On that last day, in the great banquet hall of heaven, Christ will show up and waiting will end. Can you see it? Do you long for this? Do you want to be there with Jesus right now? Are you willing to give up worrying about the cheap appetizers because you know the delightful, soul-satisfying feast that is to come?

18

Grace for Today

No matter what your circumstances, God's grace will sustain you.

Despite the warnings of her Christian parents and friends, Rachel, a Christian, married Andrew, a non-Christian. In hard moments when they didn't get along, or she goes to church alone, or she reads the Bible to her kids while her husband watches football, or when he argues with her about how to raise the kids, Rachel asks, "Where are you, God?"

No one warned Carol about marrying Frankie, even though he was such a new convert. His immaturity and tumultuous home life, combined with his volcanic anger, made for a wretched marriage. Carol often wonders, *Why didn't someone warn me marriage to Frankie would be so hard?*

After her husband Colby admitted his affair and left her, Mary was dumbfounded. She wonders, *What did I do wrong? Don't you love me, God? Is there something wrong with me that Colby would leave me for that woman?* The tears come often. For the first few months, she cried herself to sleep. In taking care of her son and returning to the workforce, Mary can barely keep up with life. She looks back and regrets that she ignored the warning signs during dating—he was a flirt and he often insisted on premarital sex. Everyone else enjoyed sex, even a number of her Christian friends, so she thought, *Who cares, so long as we get married?* But now, in the midst of her turmoil, she more than once has asked her pastor, "How could a good God do this to me?"

Rachel, Carol, and Mary are not alone. There are many women who live in agonizing situations just like them. These women ride the waves of joy and sorrow that come in difficult marriages, or in life after a divorce, and they look for God in the midst of the circumstances. Many days it's hard to see God. Too many days, it feels like he doesn't care anymore.

But God is not dead. He hasn't abandoned these women or you. God's grace is present and powerfully working, even when we don't see it. Grace is God's kindness and goodness to those who don't deserve it. Much like water and air are essential to life, God's grace is life-sustaining for a Christian. It is God's grace that takes us from darkness to light when we're first converted, and it is that very same grace that sustains believers until glory. The Christian life is all about grace.

We all deserve death because of our sins, but God, who is rich in grace and mercy, sent his Son, Jesus, to die for those who do not deserve his love. The wonder of the gospel is that for you it is free, but it came at great cost for God in giving over his Son. That's the grace of the gospel, and is God's ultimate display of love for you. God saves wretched, selfish, arrogant, foolish, immoral, manipulative, greedy, angry, and lazy people like you and me. We didn't deserve to be saved, and there is nothing we can do to earn our salvation. God saved us because his mercy and goodness is so great.

Life in a fallen world can be hard, even unbearable some days, but God's grace sustains a believer no matter the season. In the midst of suffering, the evidences of grace may be less obvious, but take heart, look closely, and you will find signs of his abundant kindness at work in your life. If you belong to Jesus, you are his beloved, and no life circumstance can change that.

Forgiving Grace

Most folks at church would have never guessed that Thomas and Samantha were sleeping together. They looked on the surface like the perfect Christian couple. They met in church and started dating quickly. Thomas initiated physical intimacy early on, and consistently transgressed forbidden boundaries, until they eventually consummated the relationship.

Samantha suffered under an enormous weight of guilt, shame, and condemnation for her actions. She had promised herself she'd wait for intimacy until marriage, but sex was exciting and it felt so good. She also craved the attention Thomas showed her. No one else asked her out, so when Thomas showed interest in her, she leapt at the opportunity and wanted to do whatever she could to keep his attention.

Samantha ran back to Jesus with her guilt. Although she knew in her head that Jesus had come as the Savior of the world to forgive sins (Luke 5:24), she struggled with feeling that her sin had put her beyond God's grasp. "I promised God I'd wait and now look at me. He must hate me," she often fretted. But, in God's grace, the words of Revelation 1:5 washed over her soul, "To him who loves us and has freed us from our sins by his blood." Her best friend, Margie, whom she confided in, reinforced this truth over and over again: "Your sin doesn't define you, God's grace does." Margie would recite the apostle Paul's words to Samantha: "Shall we go on sinning so that grace may increase? By no means! We died to sin; how can we live in it any longer?" (Romans 6:1–2 NIV). It was in this newfound forgiveness that Samantha was finally able to say "no" to Thomas, and have the strength to fight for purity.

Sanctifying Grace

Maxine and Fred grew up in church together, and though they spent their college years apart, they returned to their home church and started noticing one another. They eventually started to date, and initially, they enjoyed time with one another.

Fred had plenty of good qualities; he was responsible, charming, and thoughtful. Maxine liked him, and grew in deeper appreciation for him over time. But Fred struggled with anger. He exploded and screamed at her whenever they were alone. In conflict, curse words spilled out of his mouth. He'd rage like a bull and throw callous statements at her—"Are you really that dumb?" or "I can't believe you'd say something that stupid."

At first Maxine was scared, hurt, and confused. But eventually, she began to get entangled in his anger (Proverbs 22:24–25). She'd get drawn in and would go toe-to-toe with him in the boxing ring. There were long periods of peace, but when war broke out, it could be brutal for both of them. Maxine felt ill-equipped to deal with Fred's anger.

As disappointing as the conflict was, and ashamed as she felt for their volatile arguments, she knew that with Christ's help, she could do better. Over time, she prayed, sought accountability, grew in her faith, and learned not to respond in kind. She learned Fred's weaknesses, pet peeves, and frustrations, so she knew how to short-circuit the fights before they escalated. When he was mean, she responded with kindness and gentleness (Ephesian 4:29). Paul's words rang true for her: "Let your conversation be always full of grace" (Colossians 4:6). God's grace was evident in her life. By faith, she learned to trust God with the fights. Fred was so startled by the changes in her life, especially during conflict, that he went to their pastor for help. *If Jesus could do this for her,* he thought, *maybe he can help me, too.*

Comfort and Grace

Harry and Constance dated for several months. Her question one night threw him off guard—"Have you ever struggled with pornography?" She knew he had a past of sexual sin. He'd hinted at it, and said one day they should talk about it, but it never came up. So she took the direct approach and asked.

She was dismayed when he shared the details of his struggle. As a teenager, he had regularly watched pornography. He was a typical teenage boy whose hormones raged, and was sexually curious. His parents never told him about sex. He'd heard most of what he knew from his friends. When a scantily clad woman showed up on the computer screen in an advertisement, he clicked, and plunged into the world of porn. Now ten years later, his battle with lust, shame, and guilt continued to rage.

She couldn't bear the thought of him lusting after other women. Her insecurities, combined with the pain of his confessions, left her with no choice. With dreams of a life together shattered, she broke up with him. At first she experienced grief over the end of the relationship, especially since she thought she was going to marry Harry. The first week after the break up, the sadness was overwhelming, but God's comfort invaded the sadness. She read 2 Corinthians 1:3–4 countless times: "Blessed be the God and Father of our Lord Jesus Christ, the Father of mercies and God of all comfort, who comforts us in *all* our affliction" (emphasis added). Her mentor, an older, godly woman named Agnes, often told her, "Your despair and heartache is found in that word 'all.' God will comfort you in all your affliction." It took time, but eventually Constance believed what Agnes was saying to her, and embraced the mercy and comfort offered to her through Christ. In her grief over the lost relationship, she found God's grace poured over her life.

Sustaining Grace

Janelle met Dominique in the church nursery. She was saved in college during a season when her health tanked, and he had met Jesus at an Easter service after living a very worldly life. They often ran into each other at church, and conversations grew longer and longer. Eventually, he asked her out.

His controlling tendencies emerged a few months into the relationship. He called and texted far too often to find out where she was and who she was with. Dominique demanded that she wear certain outfits. He made her hand over her phone and checked her text messages and phone calls. If she resisted, he exploded with the force of a nuclear bomb. He held her on a tight leash, and though she disliked his tyranny, she also grew attached to him over the course of time. She loathed being single. True, he controlled her, but sex was good, he was decent to her on most days, and unlike her father, he never hit her. She might have been shopping at the bottom of a garbage can, but at least she wasn't alone anymore.

She eventually married him, and things got worse, not better. Daily doses of God's Word gave her the strength to endure in her marriage. Some seasons were miserable, but she was determined to fight for the marriage. God's grace helped her to persevere through the hard days. Dominique was rarely humble, so it required a lot from her to keep the marriage afloat. She had no choice but to pray often. When she relied on God to sustain her, she found what she needed to get up every day. It was a long, tiring road, but God's grace helped her to persevere through the hardest years.

Training Grace

Elyse dated Stephen, despite the warnings of her friends. She met him at a party. Stephen said he was a Christian, and offered to go to church with her because he found her so attractive and knew that's what she wanted to hear. However, it quickly became obvious that he was not born-again. He hadn't been to church for years, and his lifestyle showed he didn't care about the Lordship of Christ. Over time, his lifestyle spilled over into hers—sex, drinking, and some drugs. Elyse initially resisted, but step by step, he convinced her to join him—a little sex here, some drinking there, a sniff of cocaine one night, and next thing you knew, she'd strayed far from God. It was a slow but deliberate drift away from her faith.

A few close Christian friends confronted her. "You're destroying your life—you can't keep doing this." She broke down crying. She knew they were right. She broke up with Stephen immediately. She deleted his contact information from her phone and any trace of him from her Facebook and Instagram accounts.

For the first time in months, she found a grace-driven resolve to turn her life back to God. No longer did she trust herself. She entrusted herself to Christ. The apostle Paul's words became her battle cry: "For the grace of God has appeared, bringing salvation for all people, training us to renounce ungodliness and worldly passions, and to live self-controlled, upright, and godly lives in the present age, waiting for our blessed hope, the appearing of the glory of our great God and Savior Jesus Christ"

(Titus 2:11–13). She had months of bad habits stored up, but God's training grace taught her to turn her back on the drinking, sex, and drugs, and to cherish what matters much more, a hope in Christ's return. As her affections and motivations changed, so did her life. Godliness didn't come automatically, but with daily steps of obedience and with small acts of self-control, she grew in God's grace.

Trust and Grace

Stella was thirty-eight and she longed for marriage. She met Bob at a church potluck and didn't care that he was divorced. She assumed that Bob was her last chance at happiness. It had been almost ten years since a guy had asked her out on a date.

What Stella didn't tell anyone was that her life was overrun with fears. *If I don't marry Bob I'll never get married. I'll never have children. I'm going to end up as an old woman all by myself. I don't stand a chance. Who could ever love me with all my faults?* Every morning as she awoke, the worries crept in, and she struggled to push them away.

Her fears ruled her heart and plagued her mind. She clung to Bob like a scared child tightly gripping a parent and refusing to let go. Pastor Stan told her, "Trust God. The Lord is not going to abandon you," but she didn't buy it. Her years of loneliness were just too painful, and she didn't have the strength to face them anymore.

Pastor Stan asked her to read Matthew 6:19–33, where she read about laying up treasures in heaven, about not serving two masters, and about the call to abandon her lifestyle of worry. That helped some. But it was reading Psalm 56 that hit her like a tidal wave. "When I am afraid, I put my trust in you. In God, whose word I praise, in God I trust; I shall not be afraid. What can flesh do to me?" (Psalm 56:3–4). Something inside her shifted. She was still scared some days, but she grew in her trust of the Lord. She didn't want the fears to get the best of her. Whether she married Bob or not, the Lord would be at her side, even in the hard moments.

Powerful Grace

Jill and Julian were both non-Christians when they got married. Jill's father was a pastor, but she had never embraced his faith. She went to college, married a nice guy, and started what to her seemed a pretty good life.

But God slammed on the breaks. She got cancer at the young age of twenty-three. The fear of death made her search again. All the years growing up in a preacher's home hadn't changed her, but an encounter with the living Christ did. Late at night, sick from chemotherapy and exhausted from the long road to recovery, she found hope in the gospel of Matthew: "Come to me, all who labor and are heavy laden, and I will give you rest. Take my yoke upon you, and learn from me, for I am gentle and lowly in heart, and you will find rest for your souls. For my yoke is easy, and my burden is light" (11:28–30). Jesus's words washed over her like a cool breeze in a heat wave, and she never turned back. Though she had run from God, spurned the teachings of her father, and married a non-Christian man, she couldn't help but run back into the Savior's arms. It was by staring into the face of Christ that she radically came to faith in him.

Julian followed suit. Jill's conversion was so radical and so thorough, from inside out, that he couldn't help but ask, "Who is this God, who could so powerfully rescue the woman I love?" Even though her cancer treatment made her sick, and ate away at her body, her soul found refuge in Christ, and he could tell. There were many difficult days, and fears often resurfaced, but he saw a new strength in her that he had never seen before. He cracked opened a Bible, talked with the hospital chaplain, and in a matter of weeks, he had found Christ, too.

Repentance and Grace

Gloria dated Ted for six years. They had a lot in common, and really made a great team. She was outgoing, and he was more reserved. She invited folks out for dinner, and he enjoyed the company. He was more organized, and she was scatter-brained, so he would often stop by to help her organize her office or balance her checkbook.

Ted had an aversion to marriage, however. His parents divorced when he was young, and both parents had been remarried and divorced several times over. After their third year of dating, Gloria hoped they would get married, but Ted refused. He enjoyed being with her, but didn't see the point of marriage. After many years together, she had invested so much in the relationship and didn't want to let go.

Her mentor, Julie, pressed Gloria about the relationship. "If he refuses to commit, why are you hanging on to him?" Gloria made every excuse in the book—"I love him." "He's good for me and I'm good for him." "I've got too much invested in this." "Just wait, he'll come around." In the end, it was clear that she idolized Ted, and stubbornly refused to let the relationship go. She worshipped a future with Ted more than she trusted Christ.

Julie read to her 1 John 1: "If we confess our sins, he is faithful and just to forgive us our sins and to cleanse us from all unrighteousness"

(v. 9). Tears welled up in Gloria's eyes. She knew that her own stubbornness and pride were getting in the way of God's best for her. Her hard questions—like "Why, God, won't he commit?"—morphed into "I'm sorry, God, for refusing to let go." Confession of sin and owning her wrong was a sign of God's grace. It was a significant step in her walk with Christ.

A few days later, Gloria made the very difficult decision to end her relationship with Ted, despite his protests. She knew if she stayed with him, she would never get married.

Grace, Grace, and More Grace

Often when we tell our stories, we neglect to put God at the center. We are the main actors in our stories, not God. In telling the story about us, not him, we obscure our view of God's grace.

God's grace is in every storyline. It is grace that forgives, sanctifies, comforts, trains, sustains, grows trust, and powerfully transforms. These women (and men) don't get credit for making right decisions or life changes. Any good that happens comes from God (James 1:19), who willingly provides grace.

God's Word encourages us to make wise choices, and so we pray, seek counsel, go to church, and listen to sermons, all with the hope that the Spirit will guide and help us to live wisely. God's grace is found in wise choices, but his grace is also readily available when we mess up, choose poorly, and settle for the wrong guy.

Look at your life and be honest: How much do you *want* God's grace? Do you see how much you need it to thrive, let alone to survive in this fallen world? Are you desperate for his grace today?

Maybe you are facing pressure from guys or from our sex-driven culture to conform your standards. Maybe you are dating the wrong kind of guy, and you need to break up. Maybe you are coming face-to-face with sins in your own life that you must deal with. Maybe you need to find a good church, or start attending more faithfully the church you are already a part of. Maybe you are in a prolonged season of singleness, and you're hoping for God to sustain you over the long haul. Maybe you need to grow in your affections for Christ and your love for him. Maybe you are ruled by fears, loneliness, anger, or confusion about your single life. Maybe your desire for marriage has taken over your heart, or maybe you view marriage in a very healthy way. Maybe you are determined to wait for a godly man. Whatever your situation, God's grace can sustain you.

From beginning to end, through Christ, God's grace is made evident in our lives. You might not see it right now, but trust God's Word, and believe that God *is* working on your behalf. The Christian life is all about God's grace.

Conclusion: Don't Compromise

Think wisely and carefully about whom you should date and marry. It is a good thing to desire marriage, though God never guarantees it for anyone.

Don't settle for the ten wrong men I've set out in this book. *Hold out for the man who is committed to Christ, not just in his words, but with his entire life.* God's grace can sustain while you wait for a godly man. Do you believe that, or will all the fears and pressures of your life make you give up and settle for a less-than-ideal choice? Why compromise on one of the biggest decisions of your life?

Look for the guy who shows through his life that godliness matters. For some of you, that might mean choosing singleness, because that godly guy will never come around. For others, the godly guy may one day come, but for now you must wait and be patient. Whether your waiting lasts for a season, or for life, Christ will sustain you as you wait. Lean into him. He is enough for this life and for the life to come.

The goal of a Christian single woman is not to find a husband, but a Savior. The ultimate destination for Christian single women is not marriage, but heaven. Build your life around preparing for heaven by growing in your godliness and love for the Savior. You will never be disappointed.

Acknowledgments

Thanks to Barbara Juliani, Gretchen Logterman, Karen Teears, Cheryl White, and the great team at New Growth Press. Yet, again, you've given me a chance to take an idea that I've been contemplating for years, and get it into print. The editorial review of the first draft made the book much, much, much, much better. Thank you for your unending patience as I churned out a second draft.

Even more so than my other books, this has been *a team effort.* Lindsey Parker and Kristin Walberg read the introduction. Alyssa Willis looked at two initial chapters and gave me thoughtful suggestions. Pastor Blake Boylston mined the pages of Scripture with me to make sure I had ample Bible references. I'm hugely indebted to Claire Kennedy, Michelle Horton, and Li Beach—all of whom read the entire first draft and gave me dozens of useful critiques. This book is a billion times better because they carefully worked through my early manuscripts. Victoria Mwongela graciously gave her time to help me come up with the quotes at the front of every chapter. And there are countless other single and married women who answered questions to help me get into the mind and heart of single women, and to see more clearly their unending desires for marriage, children, and love.

Then, there is my very dear wife, Sarah—who keeps me sane when storms swirl around me. She edits everything I've ever written, including reading my doctoral dissertation not once, not twice, but five times over. Now if there is ever a sign of love, that's it, right? She cowrote chapter 4 in this book and made it much stronger than if I had written it on my own.

To my three daughters—Lydia, Eden, and Noelle. Foremost, this book is for the three of you. Please don't bring home the kind of guy I wrote about in this book. My prayer is that the Lord would help you to choose wisely and to avoid fools.

Endnotes

Chapter 1: Same People, New Problems

1. Joy Beth Smith, "Fat. Single. Christian. In church, being over-weight and dating feels like a sin." *Washington Post* (June 27, 2016). https://www.washingtonpost.com/news/acts-of-faith/wp/2016/06/27/fat-single-christian-in-church-being-overweight-and-dating-feels-like-a-sin/?utm_term=.afa572ebeb68.

2. National Marriage and Divorce Rate Trends, Center for Disease Control and Prevention (CDC) (November 23, 2015). http://www.cdc.gov/nchs/nvss/marriage_divorce_tables.htm.

3. Kelsey Borresen, "Five Good Reasons to Get Married While You're Young, According to Research." *Huffington Post* (November 14, 2013). http://www.huffingtonpost.com/2013/11/14/married-young_n_4227924.html.

Chapter 4: A New Direction—Living By Faith in Your Relationships

1. D. A. Carson, *The Gospel According to John*, The Pillar New Testament Commentary (Grand Rapids, MI: Eerdmans, 1991), 217–218.

2. D. A. Carson (Ed.), *Zondervan NIV Study Bible* (Grand Rapids, MI: Zondervan, 2015), 2154. Jesus often communicated spiritual truth by using physical realities from his day (light, John 1:4–5, 7–9; bread, John 6:31–51; door, John 10:1–9). Living water could refer to natural physical water, but this phrase carries obvious spiritual significance. With the other references to the Spirit in this passage, living water likely refers to eternal life through the Spirit.

3. Carson, *Zondervan NIV Study Bible*, 2156.

4. Carson, *The Gospel According to John*, 228.

Chapter 5: The Control Freak

1. John M. Gottman, *The Marriage Clinic: A Scientifically Based Marital Therapy* (New York: W.W. Norton & Company, 1999), 52–54.

2. Both examples come from Gottman, 52–54.

Chapter 6: The Promiscuous Guy

1. Garrett Kell, "How to Destroy Your Marriage Before It Begins." *The Gospel Coalition* (September 11, 2013). https://www.thegospelcoalition.org/article/how-to-destroy-your-marriage-before-it-begins.

2. D. A. Carson (Ed.), *NIV Zondervan Study Bible* (Grand Rapids: Zondervan, 2015), 2443.

3. Jamie Dunlop, "Session 8: Intimacy and Accountability," Core Seminar class at Capitol Hill Baptist Church, 3. Available at http://www.capitolhillbaptist.org/resources/core-seminars/series/singleness-courtship/ (Accessed March 5, 2016).

4. Dunlop, 3–5.

Chapter 7: The Unchurched Guy

1. Candice Watters, "What If My Boyfriend Isn't As Eager As I Am To Attend Church Activities?" *Boundless* (May 13, 2013). http://www.boundless.org/advice/2013/what-if-my-boyfriend-isnt-as-eager-as-i-am-to-attend-church-activities.

Chapter 8: The New Convert

1. Kris Swiatocho & Cliff Young, "Is It Foolish to Date a Brand New Christian?" *Crosswalk* (June 11, 2015). http://www.crosswalk.com/family/singles/he-said-she-said/is-it-foolish-to-date-a-brand-new-christian.html.

Chapter 9: The Unbeliever

1. Melody Green, "Why You Shouldn't Marry or Date an Unbeliever." *Last Days Ministries* (February 22, 2007). http://www.lastdaysministries.org/Articles/1000008652/Last_Days_Ministries/LDM/Discipleship_Teachings/Melody_Green/Why_You_Shouldnt.aspx.

2. Kathy Keller, "Don't Take It from Me: Reasons You Should Not Marry an Unbeliever." *The Gospel Coalition* (January 22, 2012). https://www.thegospelcoalition.org/article/dont-take-it-from-me-reasons-you-should-not-marry-an-unbeliever.

3. A poor way to handle 1 Corinthians 7:39 is to say it only applies to widows, as is the case in Frank Fredrick's article, "Why Marrying Unbelievers Can Work." *Huffington Post* (November 11, 2013). http://www.huffingtonpost.com/frank-fredericks/why-marrying-unbelievers-_b_4255033.html. Even though this text speaks of widows, we wouldn't restrict it to *just* widows, or else we cut out the natural application to single women. Can you imagine if we handled the rest of Scripture this way? Restricting the Bible's application only to those specifically mentioned in the Bible verse is unnecessarily restrictive of Scripture, and reduces its relevance to the Christian life.

4. Melody Green, "Why You Shouldn't Marry or Date an Unbeliever." *Last Days Ministries* (February 22, 2007). http://www.lastdaysministries.org/Articles/1000008652/Last_Days_Ministries/LDM/Discipleship_Teachings/Melody_Green/Why_You_Shouldnt.aspx.

5. Zach Schlegel, "Bringing His Holiness to Completion," Sermon on 2 Corinthians 6:14 to 7:1, Capitol Hill Baptist Church (July 26, 2015). http://www.capitolhillbaptist.org/sermon/bringing-his-holiness-to-completion/.

6. David Garland, *2 Corinthians*, vol. 29, *The New American Commentary* (Nashville: Broadman & Holman, 1999), 331.

7. The larger context of this section shows that the alliances that Paul warns against are partnerships in pagan practices (cf. 1 Corinthians 10:14–22)—unholy alliances. See Garland, 333.

8. Most everyone applies this verse to *marriage*, but if Paul is talking about a partnership or alliance with an unbeliever, why shouldn't we also say that it is unwise to *date* an unbeliever? In teaching on this verse, Mark Dever has often said that if we are not to be unequally yoked to a non-Christian then dating a non-Christian is a sin.

9. Zach Schlegel, "Things that Go Wrong in Our Courtship Culture," Core Seminar Classes at Capitol Hill Baptist Church, 4. Available at http://www.capitolhillbaptist.org/sermon/session-13-things-that-go-wrong/ (Accessed August 28, 2017).

10. Ibid.

11. Ibid.

12. Melody Green, "Why You Shouldn't Marry or Date an Unbeliever." *Last Days Ministries* (February 22, 2007). http://www.lastdaysministries.org/Articles/1000008652/Last_Days_Ministries/LDM/Discipleship_Teachings/Melody_Green/Why_You_Shouldnt.aspx.

13. Josh McDowell, *Why True Love Waits: The Definitive Book on How to Help Your Kids Resist Sexual Pressure* (Carol Streams, IL: Tyndale House, 2002), 424.

14. Melody Green, "Why You Shouldn't Marry or Date an Unbeliever." *Last Days* Ministries (February 22, 2007). http://www.lastdaysministries.org/Articles/1000008652/Last_Days_Ministries/LDM/Discipleship_Teachings/Melody_Green/Why_You_Shouldnt.aspx.

15. Ibid.

16. Ibid.

Chapter 10: The Angry Man

1. Debbie McDaniel, "10 Men Christian Women Should Never Marry." *iBelieve* (April 13, 2015). http://www.ibelieve.com/slideshows/10-types-of-men-christian-women-should-never-marry.html.

2. J. Lee Grady, "10 Men Christian Women Should Never Marry." *Charisma Magazine* (February 12, 2014). http://www.charismamag.com/blogs/fire-in-my-bones/19757-10-men-christian-women-should-never-marry.

3. The three labels for anger (divine anger, human righteous anger, human sinful anger) come from Robert D. Jones, *Uprooting Anger: Biblical Help for a Common Problem* (Phillipsburg, NJ: P & R Publishing, 2005), 18–21.

4. Tremper Longman III, *Proverbs, Baker Commentary on the Old Testament* (Grand Rapids, MI: Baker Academic, 2006), 503.

5. "Righteousness" here is not the Pauline imputed righteousness of Romans 1:16–17; but a moral, upright, faithful life. Hence, the NIV translates this "the righteous life that God desires." See Douglas Moo, *The Letter of James, The Pillar New Testament Commentary* (Grand Rapids, MI: Eerdmans, 2000), 83–84.

6. Questions 9 and 10 are based on Robert D. Jones, *Uprooting Anger*, 39.

Chapter 11: The Lone Ranger

1. C. S. Lewis, *The Four Loves* (New York: Harcourt, 1960), 169.

Chapter 12: The Commitment-Phobic Man

1. Hannah Arendt, *The Life of the Mind: The Groundbreaking Investigation in How We Think* (New York, New York: Harcourt Publishing, 1981), 165.

2. Jonathan Leeman, *The Church and the Surprising Offense of God's Love: Reintroducing the Doctrines of Membership and Discipline* (Wheaton, Illinois: Crossway, 2010), 53.

3. Ibid., 55.

Chapter 13: The Passive Man

1. Matt Walsh, "4 Things That Are Hurting Your Wife and Killing Your Marriage." *The Blaze* (December 18, 2014). http://www.theblaze.com/contributions/4-things-that-are-hurting-your-wife-and-killing-your-marriage/.

2. Ernie Baker, *Marry Wisely, Marry Well* (Wapwallopen, PA: Shepherd's Press, 2017), 26.

Chapter 14: The Unteachable Guy

1. C. S. Lewis, *God in the Dock: Essays on Theology and Ethics* (Grand Rapids: Eerdmans, 2014), 41.

2. Shelly Poston, "Warning Signs in Dating Relationships." *Christian Apologetics & Research Ministry*. https://carm.org/apologetics/womens-issues/warning-signs-dating-relationships (Accessed May 29, 2017).

Chapter 15: Breaking Up for the Glory of God

1. The first draft of this came from pastor Zach Schlegel, who wrote up our shared ideas for a class that we cotaught on dating. I've modified it and added to it for the purposes of this book.

2. This point was inspired by something I read in Sean Peron and Spencer Harmon's *Letters to a Romantic: Biblical Guidance on Dating* (Phillipsburg, NJ: P & R, 2017). Sean and Spencer let me read a pre-publication copy. The words and thoughts are my own but the idea was inspired by Spencer's "Breaking Up" chapter.

3. Ibid.

Chapter 16: In Pursuit of a Real Christian Man

1. Robertson McQuilkin, "Living by Vows." *Christianity Today* (October 8, 1990), 38-40, and Robertson McQuilkin, *A Promise Kept: The Story of Unforgettable Love* (Carol Stream, IL: Tyndale Publishing, 2006), 2–69.

2. Ibid., 2.

3. Ibid.

4. Ibid., 3.

5. Ibid., 6.

6. Robertson McQuilkin, "Ministry or Family: The Choice." *Christianity Today* (Spring 1991). http://www.christianitytoday.com/pastors/1991/spring/9112039.html.

Chapter 17: Why Is Waiting Okay?

1. Mark Dever, personal conversation about waiting.

2. Personal correspondence with Stephanie Municchi on August 30, 2016.

3. Joshua Harris, *I Kissed Dating Goodbye* (Sisters, OR: Multnomah, 1997), 75.

4. This subsection is inspired by Charles Hedman's excellent talk entitled "A Biblical Theology of Singleness," Capitol Hill Baptist Church, October 16, 2016. Available at www.capitolhillbaptist.org/sermon/a-biblical-theology-of-singleness/.

5. Mark Dever, *The Lord's Love (Psalm 33)*, Capitol Hill Baptist Church, September 18, 2016. Available at www.capitolhillbaptist.org/sermon/the-lords-love/.

6. Personal correspondence with Becca Warren on August 30, 2016.

7. Paige Benton Brown, *Singled out by God for Good. PCBC Witness* (February 1998). http://static.pcpc.org/articles/singles/singledout.pdf.

8. Dever, *The Lord's Love (Psalm 33)*.

9. Bobby Jamieson, *When Death Is Done (Isaiah 25:6–12)*, Capitol Hill Baptist Church, April 17, 2016. Available at www.capitolhillbaptist.org/sermon/when-death-is-done/.

10. Ibid.